Gods and Myths of the
Romans

Gods and Myths of the
Romans

Mary Barnett
Photography by Michael Dixon

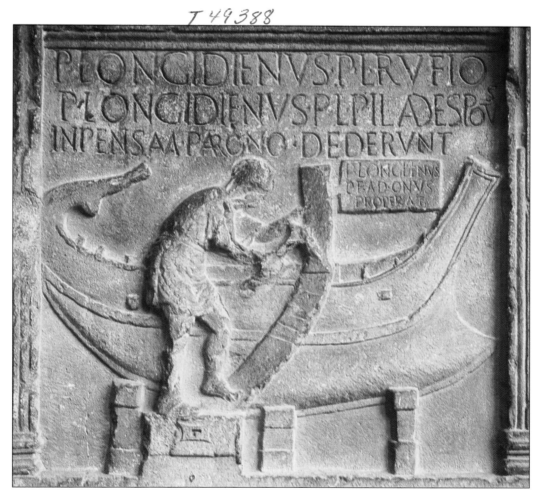

Grange
BOOKS

Published in 1999 by

Grange Books
an imprint of Grange Books PLC
The Grange
Units 1-6
Kingsnorth Industrial Estate
Hoo, Nr. Rochester
Kent
ME3 9ND

ISBN 1 84013 351 1

Printed in Singapore

*PAGE 2: The Roman Forum, with the Temple
of Saturn in the foreground, seen from the
Capitoline Hill.*

*PAGE 3: (National Museum, Ravenna) A Roman
gravestone showing a boat builder at work.*

*ABOVE: (Capitoline Museums, Rome) Head of the
Roman Emperor Constantine, from a colossal
bronze statue.*

CONTENTS

INTRODUCTION   6

CHAPTER ONE   **ROME: FROM VILLAGE TO EMPIRE**   10

CHAPTER TWO   **MYTHS OF ROME (1): THE STORY OF AENEAS**   17

CHAPTER THREE   **MYTHS OF ROME (2): THE FOUNDATION OF ROME
                    AND THE EARLY KINGS**   28

CHAPTER FOUR   **DOMESTIC RELIGION AND THE EARLY GODS
                    OF ROME**   41

CHAPTER FIVE   **STATE RELIGION IN REPUBLICAN ROME**   49

CHAPTER SIX   **THE INTRODUCTION OF NEW GODS INTO
                    REPUBLICAN ROME**   59

CHAPTER SEVEN   **THE GODS OF THE ROMAN EMPIRE**   79

CHAPTER EIGHT   **ROME AND CHRISTIANITY**   94

                    INDEX   108

INTRODUCTION

It is often said that the Romans had no myths. In the sense that myths are significant traditional stories concerning supernatural beings or historical or natural phenomena, this appears at first sight to be true. Yet it seems unbelievable that such stories should not have grown up among the early Latins in the same way that they did among other people. Roman literature and art, however, show mere traces of native myths that are almost impossible to identify and dislodge from the Greek literary tradition that absorbed and changed them.

Myths usually originate from an oral tradition, in which they are handed down from one generation to another. Sometimes such myths come to the surface and are frozen for posterity when they are gathered up and written down while they are still current, as they seem to have been in Greece by Homer, for example, who in the eighth century set down myths that had probably been told there since the Bronze Age.

Rome arrived on the scene too late for this to happen. When the works of Homer were being written, Rome was nothing more than a collection of huts on a hill near the Tiber. Once the city had become powerful it took its place in a world whose culture had been overwhelmingly Hellenistic since the conquests of Alexander in the fourth century BC. There were Greek kings and Greek cities in the east from Asia Minor to Afghanistan, in Egypt, and of course in Greece itself. From as early as the eighth century BC, Greek colonists had settled round the southern coast of Italy, and in coastal areas of Sicily.

All these cities shared a language, the *koine*, or common language, of Greece that had superseded its earlier dialects. The culture of their rich and educated classes was Greek. A particular feature of that culture was its taste for explaining the foreign cultures it dominated in terms of its own myths, for superimposing its own kind of stories on the stories of other people. Later Greek writers even suppressed local myths completely and invented new ones of their own to explain some local incident or phenomenon. For example, elements from the Greek myths about the god Dionysus were imposed on stories about the Egyptian god, Osiris, and even on stories about the Buddha. Sometimes, in their urge to make a good story, they turned local deities into people, as we shall see.

It seems likely that traditional oral myths and legends once existed among the Latin tribes who were the first inhabitants of Rome. If so, they were lost before the Romans developed the art of writing. Instead, their remnants were written down and re-interpreted later by Greek writers in their own tradition. Once Rome became an important city, its own educated classes were also Hellenized. They might have thought little of the Greek ability for practical affairs, but they aspired to the Greek culture of the Mediterranean and Near Eastern world.

The gods of the Romans were, in fact, probably never surrounded by the same kind of myths as the gods of the Greeks because the Romans seem to have perceived their gods in a way that was unusual in Europe at that period. The early Romans were still essentially animists, that is they responded to the sacred power within natural and man-made objects. It was the *numen*, or powerful spirit, of each deity that was important to the Romans, and the function that it was able to perform or withhold according to its disposition. Consequently the Romans were concerned with man's ability to hold himself in a mutually stable and profitable relationship with all the gods. They did not, at first, perceive their gods in human form, as the Greeks did, and therefore did not supply them with families and histories. What mattered to the Romans was not stories about the gods, but their powers and the dutiful and proper manner by which man might propitiate them and so maintain the all-important *pax deorum* or peace of the gods. Briefly, Romans seem to have been more interested in the function of a god than in his personality. It was inevitable, therefore, that when poets and artists wished to express their religion in mythical, anthropomorphic terms, they turned to Greek models.

The myths that have become essentially Roman are not to do with gods but with the history of Rome. These have been called, quite justly, 'pseudo-myths' because they were, for the most part, deliberately created by writers, usually Greek ones, rather than evolving gradually from a native folk tradition. They are foundation-legends, stories about the origin and early development of the city itself and it is almost possible to watch the myth of the foundation and early history of Rome developing over the centuries to suit the people for whom it was told.

The first historians of Rome of whom we are aware wrote in the third century BC in Greek. Since traditional Greek myths and legends represented history for educated Romans, it was natural that they were not averse to having their city placed in that tradition. In spite of the fact that a native foundation myth of Romulus and Remus, which will be considered later, was already current, Greek writers pushed the story of the origin of Rome further back into their own cultural past by developing the tale of Aeneas, the Trojan who, with his young son, had escaped from the sack of Troy, bearing his father on his shoulders.

Various stories of the later travels of Aeneas had been current in the Greek world for a long time, and at some stage it became clear that his destiny had been to travel to Italy, where he founded a Latin town, Lavinium, from which his son would found Alba Longa, near Rome, thirty years later. A long line of Alban kings then had to be invented to account for the many years that elapsed between the Greek story of Aeneas, which followed on from the Trojan war, and the Roman story of the founding of Rome by Romulus, which was traditionally thought to have happened in 753 BC.

The stories of Aeneas and Romulus and the early kings and heroes of Rome form what became essentially the myth of Rome. They are not myths in the strict sense of the word, but they became myths for the Roman people in the sense that they embodied the high ideals and values to which they referred over the centuries when they wanted to explain to themselves what it was to be Roman. It is a legitimate function of myth to create patterns that help people understand why things are as they are. In this way, the stories of Aeneas and Romulus may have been deliberate creations, but they could be said to have assumed mythical status over years of repetition and reference.

For mythical stories about the gods, the reader should turn to books about the myths of Greece and simply relate a Roman god to the stories told about his or her Greek equivalent. The equivalents are set out and explained later in this book, but there has seemed no point here in repeating the stories, which were not in any sense Roman, and which are readily available elsewhere.

The Capitol, seen from the Forum, at Ostia Antica, the port of Ancient Rome.

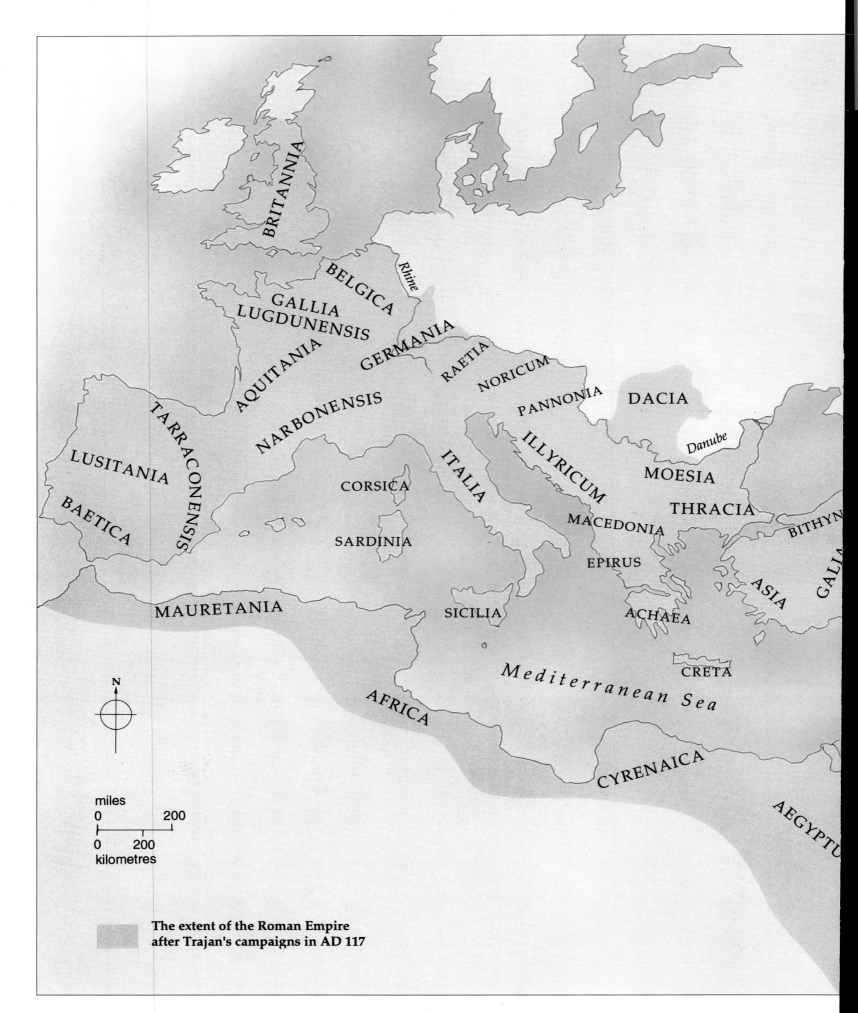

The extent of the Roman Empire
after Trajan's campaigns in AD 117

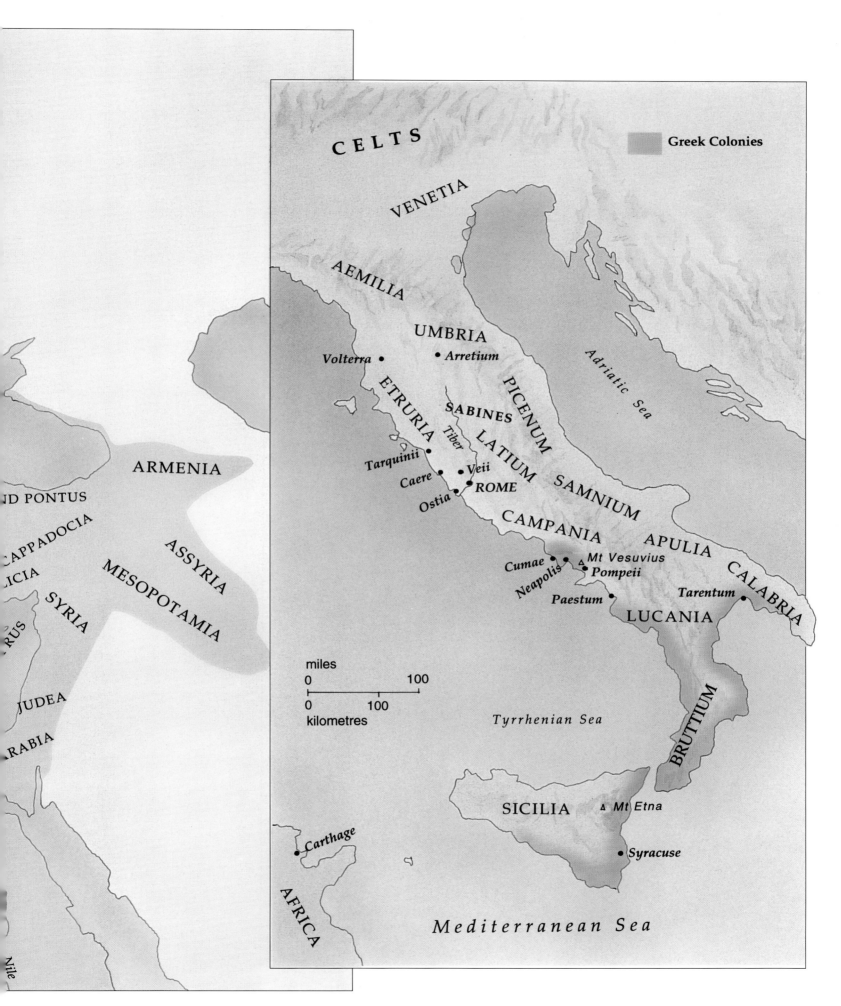

CELTS

Greek Colonies

VENETIA

AEMILIA

UMBRIA

Volterra •   • *Arretium*

ETRURIA

SABINES

PICENUM

Adriatic Sea

Tiber

LATIUM

Tarquinii •

Caere •   • *Veii*

• ROME

Ostia •

SAMNIUM

APULIA

CAMPANIA

CALABRIA

Cumae •   • △ *Mt Vesuvius*

Neapolis •   • *Pompeii*

Paestum •   • *Tarentum*

LUCANIA

miles

0   100

0   100

kilometres

Tyrrhenian Sea

BRUTTIUM

SICILIA   △ *Mt Etna*

Carthage •

• *Syracuse*

AFRICA

Mediterranean Sea

ARMENIA

ND PONTUS

CAPPADOCIA

ASSYRIA

ICIA

MESOPOTAMIA

RUS

SYRIA

JUDEA

RABIA

Nile

CHAPTER ONE
ROME: FROM VILLAGE TO EMPIRE

The gods and myths of Ancient Rome developed with and helped to define and sustain the Roman Empire. A settlement of farmers near the river Tiber in Italy grew into a city that gradually united and led all the peoples of Italy, then spread its rule across Europe and the Mediterranean world north-west as far as the border with the Scots, south-west through the Iberian peninsula, across the Mediterranean and along the North African coast to Egypt, as far east as Syria and Asia Minor, and north to the Elbe. The period from the origin of Rome until the end of its western empire was about eleven hundred years, while its eastern empire survived, though latterly in a weakened state, for about two thousand years.

During this long period the Romans maintained some of their own early cults, sometimes without remembering their origins; but they also absorbed cults from their neighbours and from the people they traded with or ruled over and, in many cases, they assimilated their own gods to foreign ones who seemed to have similar functions or powers. The extraordinarily flexible and tolerant polytheism of the Romans survived as an established state religion until 313 BC when the Emperor Constantine put in motion changes that allowed Christianity to take its place.

They were particularly influenced by the religious and cultural traditions of Greece that were already well established and had been shaped into a coherent literary and artistic form by the time Rome became a city of any consequence. But because there were so many influences on the gods and myths of Rome, it is necessary to begin with a brief account of what is now known about the origin and development of the city, and to summarize the expansion of its empire before looking at the myths that grew up to explain the phenomenon of Rome and the gods the Romans worshipped.

The geographical position of Rome was of prime importance to its history. The Alps divide Italy from Europe in the north then, beyond the Po Valley, the peninsular has a mountainous spine, formed by the Apennines, that leaves a relatively narrow, dry coastal plain on the eastern, Adriatic side of the country, and a relatively wide, fertile plain on the western, Tyrrhenian side, where the mountains slope down into the plains of Latium and Campania and into hilly, but fertile, Etruria. As the Apennines run almost due south into Lucania and Calabria, the 'toe' of the peninsula, they leave another plain, Apulia, in the 'heel' on the eastern side.

Only the rivers Po, Arno and Tiber have ever been seriously navigable, and there are very few bays or potential harbours along the shallow Tyrrhenian coast. Land routes have to find their way through the hills and mountains, usually following river valleys.

Rome lies about half way down the western coast, about 15 miles (24 km) inland, at the lowest point at which the Tiber can be crossed, where there is also an island in the river. It happens that this position was, and is still, a junction of the major land routes through the hills and along the coast, routes that once included the salt route to the eastern moun-

tains. Grouped near the flood plain of the Tiber are certain low, volcanic hills, some of which have sheer, defensive sides. These would have provided dry settlements above the flood plain. Clearly this was a very desirable position, but one for which there would have been competition.

Archaeologists have found evidence of Neolithic and Bronze Age cultures in Etruria and Latium, the central areas of Italy with which we are concerned. It was not until the early Iron Age, however, that Italy began to show signs of developing in any way that could be compared to the civilizations further east in Greece and Asia Minor. In the early Iron Age a culture known as Villanovan, from the town of Villanova near Bologna, on which it was centred, appeared in the Po Valley, then in Etruria and Latium, whence it spread further south. This was succeeded by the more highly developed urban culture of the Etruscans, whose origin is still debated; some scholars think they came from Asia Minor, others from northern Europe. Whatever their origin, their language was not Indo-European and some of their texts have proved resistant to translation. They began to move into the central area of the peninsula by about 700 BC, and exercised a great deal of influence on surrounding cultures until about the fourth century BC.

From the middle of the eighth century BC Greek colonists began to settle in what came to be known as 'Magna Graecia', an area round the southern coast of Italy and the coast of Sicily, where they founded cities such as Cumae, Tarentum, Catania and

Syracuse, which in their turn founded other important cities: Selinus (Selinunte), Neapolis (Naples), Paestum and Agrigento, for example. The cultural influence of Greece on the rest of Italy was very important, particularly on the Etruscans, with whom they had early contacts.

In the centre of Italy, between the two powerful groups of Etruscans in the north and Greeks in the south, lived a divided population made up of groups having an extraordinarily diverse mixture of ethnic, linguistic, social, economic and religious identities. These included the Latins in Latium, on the coast, and the Sabines and Umbrians in the interior.

It seems likely that Rome itself began as a Latin settlement in about the middle of the eighth century BC. Archaeologists have discovered traces of Iron Age hut dwellings of this date on the Palatine, one of the hills overlooking the Tiber, and evidence of graves in the plain below the hill, which later became the Forum, of a slightly earlier date. There is also evidence for slightly later dwellings on the Esquiline and Quirinal hills. This evidence all suggests that Rome began in the eighth century as a hill settlement of farmers, probably shepherds, who had their cemetery in the plain below. Thus it was comparable with other Iron Age settlements scattered through the

Remains of the Greek city of Selinunte in Sicily, showing the remains of Temple C on the Acropolis.

plain of Latium, but very different from Etruscan cities to the north, Greek cities to the south, and the mountainous homes of surrounding tribes.

Other villages came into being on the hills around the plain and gradually linked themselves together, as many Latin communities did, until by about 650 BC Rome was probably a small Latin town. It continued to grow slowly for the next hundred years, during which time the meeting place, or Forum, was drained and no longer used as a cemetery. Archaeological evidence suggests that between about 550-475 BC there was a great spurt of development, which probably coincided with a period of Etruscan rule in the town. Evidence of walls, drains and monuments and fragments of Greek pottery and Etruscan painted terracotta ware date from this period. Remains have been found of temples, most importantly the great Capitoline temple that was dedicated in 509 BC to the triad of gods, Jupiter, Juno and Minerva. It seems likely that by the time the Etruscan rulers left Rome and retreated to their own territory further north in about 475 BC, Rome was a large city spread over several hills, surrounded by a wall, and ornamented with a number of sanctuaries to the gods of Latium and Etruria.

Roman tradition is probably correct in saying that the city was ruled by kings in the early period since kingship was the normal system of rule among the local tribes then. Throughout central Italy there was, however, a decline in rule by kings at the end of the sixth century BC, and administrative and religious power began instead to reside in the hands of colleges of magistrates, elected from aristocratic families. The histories of Rome written in the first century BC give 509 BC as the date of the end of its monarchy and the beginning of republican rule. Modern scholars suggest that it was probably as much as twenty five years later than this; but in any case a Republic can be said to have settled in by 450 BC, in a more painstaking and less dramatic fashion than the myths about Rome suggest. It took the form of government by two consuls, elected annually by the aristocratic ruling group.

Once the Republic was established, it was forced to take notice of the fact that, although the geographical position of the city was favoured, it was also tempting to invaders both from the interior and from the Mediterranean basin – from Sicily, Carthage and Sardinia. Roman literature suggests that the city's rulers never lost the sense of being vulnerable and beleaguered. They had to be strong to discourage threats to their security. It seems likely, therefore, that subsequent expansion began chiefly as an active response to a perceived threat.

Rome was by this time already a mixture of Latins and Sabines who had been strongly influenced by Etruscan civilization. One period of rule by Etruria was, however, felt to be enough, and the city saw the nearby Etruscan city of Veii as a constant threat. Rome gradually worked towards removing such threats by a well-judged mixture of war and diplomacy. Etruscan power was already waning by about 400 BC, and in 396 BC Rome succeeded in destroying Veii and annexing its territory. After that it used diplomacy in its relations with other Etruscan cities and managed to contain the power of Etruria while leaving its cities free to continue their normal industrial and commercial life.

Celtic tribes had been pressing down the eastern side of Italy since the fifth century BC, and in 390 there was a Gallic raid on Rome, which weakened the city's influence on its Latin allies by suggesting that it was vulnerable. Yet it was a raid for plunder rather than possession and in the long term served to stimulate Rome to greater efficiency. The Servian Wall was built round the city, and the army learned better defensive strategies. New officials were created to handle the affairs of the expanding state, and by 348 BC Rome was strong enough to enter into a treaty with Carthage, the great trading city on the coast of what is now Tunisia.

After fighting a war against her former allies, Rome was in a sufficiently strong position to organize Latium under her leadership, using a system that she later employed successfully much further afield. Rome became the political centre of the area without actually centralizing her rule. She allowed

autonomy to the cities she was responsible for, but asked in return that they should follow her foreign policy and provide troops for her army in emergencies. She thus ensured that other cities would combine with her in mutual defence against an aggressor.

Rome gradually extended this system to the cities of Campania, where the Greek cities also accepted a flexible system that allowed them to live their own life except in time of war. In order to secure strategic positions in neighbouring regions, Rome set up a system of colonization by which land was given to retired soldiers in return for their past service. The colonies were adapted to local circumstances, but clearly brought Roman influence to distant areas without terrorizing or even dominating them. The city could fight brutally at times, however, and after such occasions took the remaining population as slaves. By this combination of procedures Rome gradually united Italy, building roads and sometimes aqueducts in the process. The city thus built up a confederacy in Italy, which gave special privileges to the Latins.

This confederacy was clearly a power to be reckoned with, and one that was perceived as a threat by Carthage, which at that time controlled western Sicily as well as Sardinia and part of Spain. In 264 BC a minor incident caused the first of three major wars between Rome and Carthage; these are known as the Punic Wars from the Latin word for Phoenician since the Carthaginians were Phoenician in origin. Rome entered the First Punic War (264-241 BC) almost by accident, but then had to address the problem seriously, which she did by establishing a fleet and learning how to fight at sea in order to defeat Carthage. Having driven the Carthaginians from Sicily, Corsica and Sardinia, and after intensely destructive campaigns by both sides, Rome won the war and found herself in possession of her first overseas provinces.

The Second Punic War (218-201 BC) affected the population of Italy more directly since the great Carthaginian general Hannibal invaded their country expecting local Italian tribes to support him against Rome; he was disappointed in this, however, which suggests that the Roman system of confederation was working successfully. Hannibal had a great victory at Cannae in Apulia, where probably more than 30,000 people were killed, and at this the Romans despaired. Nevertheless they continued to pour men and resources into the war, which extended into Spain, Sicily and North Africa, until Hannibal was finally defeated at Zama and negotiated a settlement between Carthage and Rome.

Throughout the wars, Rome was able to rely on the support of the Italians, while Carthage on the contrary had very little manpower on which it could rely. This foreshadowed the future strength of the Romans, which always lay in its armies. As a result of the war, Rome had gained two more provinces in Spain. Later, after the Third Punic War, which ended in 146 BC, Rome destroyed the city of Carthage utterly and took her territory, which she ruled as the Province of Africa. Rome then dominated the western Mediterranean.

Response to a threat followed by prolonged, determined, destructive but ultimately professional and successful warfare, became a pattern in the development of Roman power. To the east, she was drawn successfully into the Macedonian Wars in 197 BC, but did not expand her direct rule there until she claimed Macedonia as a province in 146 BC. When King Attalus of Pergamum died in 133 BC he bequeathed his kingdom to Rome, and it became the province of Asia. Rome went to the help of the friendly city of Massilia (Marseilles), defeated the Gaulish tribes who were threatening it, and consequently absorbed southern Gaul in the process. When Mithridates of Pontus threatened Rome, the brilliant general Pompey took Pontus, Syria and Cyprus as provinces. In the 50s Julius Caesar fought the constantly threatening Gauls in the north of Italy and at last incorporated Cisalpine Gaul into the rest of Italy.

Thus, during the period of the Republic, Rome can be said to have become controller of the whole Mediterranean region either directly or through the exercise of influence over native rulers. This expansion was not without problems, however. The Roman army was drawn from the free peasant class, and it has been estimated that such men spent about seven years of their lives in the army, during which time their care and labour was withdrawn from the land they normally farmed. Meanwhile, Roman victories abroad resulted in thousands of conquered slaves being sent back to the city. As the ruling families in Rome grew rich through such offices as arranging contracts for supplies to the army, they invested in large, landed estates, which they then ran with the free labour of slaves. Thus the returning peasant soldier found he had lost his land to the upper classes and his work to the slaves he had helped to create. This lead to unrest and political struggles in Rome itself. By this time the city was overcrowded, unhealthy, full of poor people who had flocked there from the countryside, and ruled by men drawn from a limited group of families, many of whom had succumbed to the temptations of profitable office.

Military campaigns were lead by men from the ruling group who were elected by their fellow senators. Increasingly, the power of men who led successful campaigns abroad became a threat to the stability of the Republic at home. There was a strong tradition of annual elections to high office, but military campaigns sometimes lasted for several years, during which a successful leader could accumulate reputation, honour and popularity. The success of men like Sulla, Pompey and Julius Caesar led eventually to civil wars.

After his brilliant campaigns in Gaul, where he was Governor for two long terms, the great military leader, Julius Caesar, crossed the river Rubicon in the north and made it clear that he was invading his own country, but he then interspersed war with rival leaders at home with successful campaigns in Asia Minor, Africa and Spain. Once in power in Rome, he instituted many reforms – political, social and administrative – in Rome itself and in the Roman army. Instead of being consul for a year in the accepted fashion, however, he acted like a king. He refused the title *rex*, or king, but showed little regard for the political institutions of the republic. His murder in 44 BC was probably inevitable for these reasons. It led to a renewed struggle for power and yet more civil wars. These ended when Octavian, or Gaius Julius Caesar Octavianus, great-nephew and adopted heir of Julius Caesar, defeated the combined forces of Mark Antony and Cleopatra at Actium in 31 BC, thus conquering his Roman rival and bringing Egypt under Roman control.

Octavian was now in control of the Roman Empire, and in 27 BC he accepted the title of Augustus, under which he ruled as a constitutional *princeps*, or first citizen, until his death in AD 14. His rule, which with hindsight we notice coincided with the birth of Christ, was also a turning point in Roman history, as it marked the beginning of the period of Empire in the sense that he arranged that one of his family should succeed him as emperor after his death and so brought to an end the republican period and introduced a new régime that lasted for several hundred years. He himself was a reforming and popular ruler with great administrative powers, who tactfully chose to live a relatively austere life.

The rule of Augustus is particularly significant to the study of the gods and myths of Rome because, following a long and chaotic period of civil unrest, he deliberately instituted a return to what he perceived as the true Roman tradition in religion, morality and government. Festivals and cult rites that had long been neglected were revived, and temples and sanctuaries renewed. His ideals were propagated successfully by a brilliant group of poets and prose writers who lived in Rome at that time. Above all, it is from the poetry of Virgil and Horace and the prose of Livy that we derive our sense of what it was to be Roman. Ovid, who retold the Greek myths so vividly and gracefully did not, however, meet with approval and, possibly for reasons of morality, was banished from Rome.

Under Augustus, the frontiers of the Empire were settled at a point he felt was far enough, and for many years after his death the *Pax Romana*, or Roman Peace, prevailed in the Empire, with the western part dominated by Latin culture and the

(Museum of Pagan Art, Arles) A Roman portrait bust of a young Octavian, who later became the Emperor Augustus.

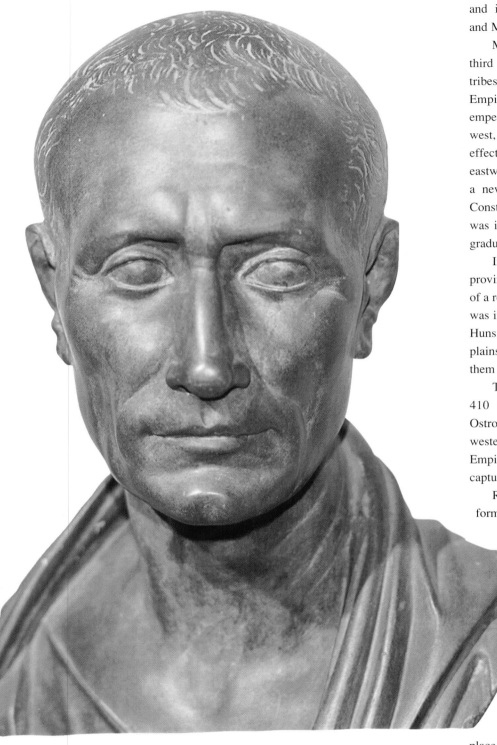

(Vatican Museums) A vivid Roman portrait bust of Julius Caesar.

and included the provinces of Armenia, Assyria and Mesopotamia.

More had to be done in the second half of the third century to stem incursions by Goths and other tribes across the northern and eastern frontiers of the Empire. By AD 284, when Diocletian became emperor, he split the empire into two parts, east and west, in order that it should be supervised more effectively. Gradually the centre of gravity shifted eastwards, until the Emperor Constantine established a new, Christian, capital at Byzantium, renamed Constantinople, in AD 330. After this, although it was in theory governed by joint rulers, the Empire gradually split into two halves.

In their weakened state, the Empire's outlying provinces were attacked by invaders, who were part of a relentless surge of tribes, whose tidal movement was initially set in motion by a nomadic people, the Huns, when they migrated from their home on the plains of central Russia, pushing other tribes before them as they went purposefully forward.

The city of Rome was sacked by Visigoths in 410 and by Vandals in 455, and in 493 the Ostrogoths established a kingdom in Italy. Thus the western empire fell to the invaders. The Byzantine Empire survived, however, until Constantinople was captured by the Turks in 1453.

Roman influence survived in the West in the form of the 'romance', or Roman, languages of France, Spain and Italy, in law and in engineering feats such as roads and bridges.

Of all its religions, the last arrival, Christianity, survived into the 'Holy Roman Empire' whose Pope was called *Pontifex Maximus* just as the chief priest of pagan Rome had been.

This very simplified survey of an extremely complex period is intended to suggest the mass of influences that must have worked on Roman perceptions of their place in the world, and on the kind of gods they needed to placate. How did religious ceremony help them? What myth of Roman greatness sustained its soldiers and its citizens? These are some of the questions we shall try to answer in the following pages.

eastern part by Greek culture in the form of the Hellenism that followed the earlier conquests of Alexander the Great.

The period from about AD 70-235 is generally agreed to have been the high point of the Empire. The province of Britain had been added after Claudius's invasion in AD 43, but nothing more until in AD 101-02 and 106, Trajan's wars in Dacia, that had begun as a defence of the northern frontier, were so successful that he added the kingdom of Daciato to the Empire. At the end of Trajan's reign, in AD 117, the Empire had reached its greatest extent,

CHAPTER TWO
MYTHS OF ROME (1): THE STORY OF AENEAS

The aristocracy of Rome set great store by tradition and by the genealogies of their own families. They are likely to have recorded the genealogies by telling them over from one generation to the next. The leading *gentes*, or families, of Rome were important because they virtually governed the state between them. They looked for their traditions, as people often do, in a past that never actually existed. Unusually, they recreated this past in a form that had the appearance of comparatively sober history rather than myth or folklore.

Their heroic men and women were perhaps unusual too in that they displayed, first and foremost, certain moral qualities that created a set of values against which their descendants could measure themselves for all time. Roman heroes were not simply brave but acted as patterns or examples of endurance and loyalty and dutiful and proper Roman behaviour in relation to the gods and the state.

Yet the first histories of Rome were written not by Romans but by Greeks, and they attempted to fit Rome into their own cultural tradition. One means of doing this was to use the story of Aeneas's wanderings after the Trojan War to provide an early precursor of the founding of Rome. The hero was then made thoroughly Roman when the story was retold by Virgil in the time of Augustus.

As we have seen, Rome probably actually emerged as a real city late in the sixth century BC. In Greece, Homer's *Iliad*, which told the story of the Trojan War, had probably been in existence for two hundred years by then. It was an inspired and pow-

erfully written version of already existing oral myths, legends and genealogies, dealing with events that probably happened in the Bronze Age.

Homer says that the god Poseidon intervened to save one of the Trojan heroes for a greater future. This was Aeneas, the son of Anchises and the goddess Aphrodite – Venus to the Romans – who escaped from the sack of Troy, holding his son by the hand and bearing his father on his shoulders. Some scholars actually think this episode might have been added to the poem at a later date to account for the gradual development of the story of Aeneas.

Illustrations on Athenian vases found in Etruria tell us that the story of Aeneas was already known there in the sixth century BC, and various versions of Aeneas's search for a new home after the Trojan War appear in both Greek and Latin literature, as do stories of Greek veterans of the Trojan War who, finding no welcome at home after a ten-year absence, settled in Sicily and on the southern Italian coast. These stories, of course, were typical foundation myths, designed to give historical significance to the leading families of Magna Graecia, the areas of Italy and Sicily colonized by the Greeks. The end of the Trojan War was clearly seen as a time of the dispersal and wandering of the great Bronze Age heroes and therefore as an opportunity to claim them as founders of new cities and respectable new genealogies in the west.

The story of Aeneas was told most memorably and completely in the age of Augustus in an epic poem by Virgil (Publius Virgilius Maro). It deliberately set out to create a myth about the origins of Rome, and it worked. Virgil was born in the north of Italy near Mantua in Cisalpine Gaul, a city that still had a strong Etruscan tradition. He first lived in Rome at the age of 16. Augustus urged him to write the poem to celebrate Rome under his rule, and it developed into a national epic, in twelve books, which sets out the Roman virtues through the portrait of its hero. It does not glorify Rome in a brazenly triumphalist manner but with discretion, stressing the need for duty as well as victory. Because it is set in the distant past it suggests, through its hero, the difficulties that had to be overcome before Rome was able to achieve the glory that culminated in the rule of Augustus.

It is humane, moving and beautifully written. It creates a mythical past, partly by following the Homeric style of allowing certain gods to speak throughout as participants in the drama. By Virgil's time the Romans had assimilated their own deities to the Greek gods and they were thus able to appear as characters in the drama in a way the early Roman divinities, who were simply spirits, would not have been. It also follows Homer's pattern by having set pieces in which warrior heroes fight to the death. It departs from Homer in portraying its hero throughout as a man whose significance lies in the future. He is seen as the ancestor of Augustus through the Julian family. Virgil also uses a device by which various characters from the past within the poem make important prophetic speeches that prompt the reader to look forward to the greatness of the Augustan age. He praises Augustus discreetly by this method and at the same time places him in the context of a heroic past.

Because the Trojan War happened long before the creation of Rome, Virgil shows that Aeneas founded an earlier city, and that it was his son's heirs who would found Rome itself. What he could not have known is that his poem created a new myth through its own power. This was ironic since it had not been perfected when he died, and he is said to have asked for it to be destroyed.

The hero of the Aeneid is often described as *pius* Aeneas; the word pious in Latin has the sense of 'dutiful to the gods', a quality highly valued in Rome. Throughout his adventures Aeneas subjects himself to the will of the gods, although sometimes reluctantly. In this, he acts as a pattern of behaviour, displaying the pre-eminent Roman virtues.

We first meet him and his emigrant Trojans at sea, wearily searching for a new land in which to settle, 'so hard and huge a task it was to found the Roman people.' Early in the poem we learn that the goddess Juno (Hera in Greek mythology) is the implacable enemy of all Trojans, partly because the Trojan prince Paris did not choose her as the most beautiful goddess, and she will do all she can to prevent the Trojans founding a new city that will one day come into conflict with the city she favours, Carthage. In her jealous fury, she causes the Trojan fleet to be shipwrecked on a Libyan shore.

After the storm, Venus (the Greek Aphrodite), who Greek myths tell us is the mother of Aeneas, questions the great god Jupiter (Greek Zeus) about her son's fate. Jupiter explains to her, and us, that Aeneas will fight a massive war in Italy, then rule for three years in a new city in Latium. His son Ascanius, who was also called Ilus while he lived in Ilium – another name for Troy – will now have Iulus instead as his second name. In this way Virgil links the descendants of Aeneas with the Julian family, from which came Julius Caesar and his nephew Octavian, later Augustus.

Ascanius/Iulus, will have power for thirty years, but will transfer his capital to Alba Longa. That city will be ruled for three hundred years by descendants of Trojans until its priestess, Ilia, bears twins to the god Mars. They will be brought up by a she-wolf and one of them, Romulus, will found the city of Rome itself. For the Romans, says Jupiter, 'I set no limits, world or time, but make the gift of Empire without end,' and from them will come the 'Trojan Caesar'. The words of Jupiter therefore set Aeneas into the context of the traditional history of Rome's foundation and show that he is the pre-ordained precursor of that city, not its actual founder, and that he was the forefather of Augustus.

Venus appears to Aeneas on the Libyan shore as a beautiful young huntress. He recognizes her as a goddess but sadly not, until just before she disappears, as his mother. When he complains to her of his fate, she tells him the story of the local queen Dido who, like Aeneas, has been forced from her home. Dido and her followers left Phoenicia after her brother, the Prince of Tyre, killed her husband, and they are building a new city of Carthage in Africa.

Virgil thus draws a comparison between the origins of Carthage and Rome, although he makes the foundation of Carthage mythically contemporary with the end of the Trojan War, instead of more accurately with the actual foundation of Rome. Juno's partiality for Carthage enables Virgil to suggest that divine intervention was responsible for the enmity between the two cities that exploded in the Punic Wars whose horrors were still remembered in Rome in his day.

When Aeneas meets the beautiful Dido, he tells her his story, rather in the manner in which Odysseus recounts the tale of his wanderings in Homer's *Odyssey*. Aeneas begins with the sack of Troy and the death of his wife, Creusa, who later came to him as a spirit and forbade him to mourn, foretelling his long exile and his future settlement 'on Hesperia where Lydian Tiber flows', where he would marry and found a kingdom.

He describes how he set off from burning Troy with his father, his son Ascanius, his people and his 'hearth gods and the greater gods'. The carrying of his gods to Italy was a crucial part of the story in many of its versions, and may have been an important reason for its first having been told, as an explanation of a cult-transfer from one region to another. Like many Greek heroes before him, Aeneas made for the island of Delos to consult the oracle of Apollo about where he should take his people. The oracle told him to 'look for your mother of old.' Old Anchises, the father of Aeneas, immediately interpreted the motherland as meaning Crete because Teucris, the forefather of the Trojans, had set off

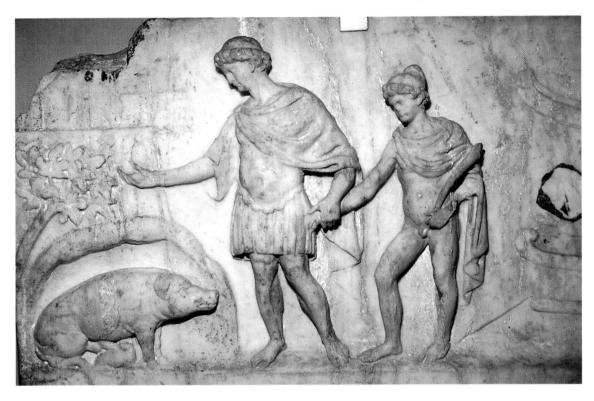

from there to found Troy in the far distant past.

After a short stay on Crete, the Trojan exiles fell sick with a plague. On this occasion Aeneas's household gods appeared to him at night and explained that Hesperia, the land he must make for, was actually Italy; it was the Trojans' true home from which their forefathers, Dardanus and Iasdius, had originated.

The Trojans set off again, and landed on one of the Strophades islands, where they slaughtered some unattended cattle to sacrifice and eat. They were prevented from eating by an instant attack by Harpies, monstrous bird-women from Greek myth, who swooped on the food and fouled what they did not carry off. When Aeneas's men attacked them, the leading Harpy prophesied that, as punishment, the Trojans would find Italy but would not create their city until hunger had made them eat their very plates.

Their next landfall was Epirus where, to their pleasure, they found that Helenus, a surviving son of King Priam of Troy, was now ruler. He told Aeneas that when he reached Italy he must look out for a giant white sow suckling thirty snow-white piglets. This detail suggests that the story is of quite a late date since it seems to be intended to symbolize the fact that thirty was the number of cities in the Latin League. Aeneas would find the sow on the further coast of Italy. On his way there, he must stop at Cumae to visit the Sibyl, a prophetess who would tell him more.

Aeneas landed first in Sicily, at Drepanum near Eryx, where there was a shrine to his mother, Venus.

Virgil is here making both a mythological and a tactfully political point, since the shrine had originally been made to the Phoenician goddess, Astarte, who was assimilated to their goddess Aphrodite by the Greek colonists in Sicily, and who was then identified with Venus in Roman times. Since Homer claimed in the *Iliad* that Aeneas was the son of Aphrodite (Venus), Virgil can be seen here to be emphasizing his hero's cultural and genealogical links with much of the Mediterranean world.

To the sorrow of all, old Anchises died in Sicily. When the Trojans continued their journey, they were shipwrecked on the Libyan shore after passing many dangers, such as Scylla and Charybdis and Polyphemus the one-eyed giant, that Homer had described Odysseus encountering earlier.

Dido listened to these stories with wonder and was consumed with a fierce love for Aeneas. Venus and Juno together had fanned the flame of her love, Venus because she wanted to protect her son from further harm and give him a beautiful wife, and Juno because she wanted to ensure that Aeneas would stay in Carthage so that Rome would never come into being. The next part of the poem, Book VI, tells Dido's tragic story, and has in itself become a powerful myth of betrayed love.

One bright day Dido and Aeneas went hunting together, but Juno raised a storm from which the couple took shelter in a cave. Goddess and nymphs were on hand to witness the 'marriage' of Dido and Aeneas in the cave, and from that time Dido 'thought no longer of a secret love but called it marriage.'

Aeneas responded to her love and seemed to forget his mission, dressing in Phoenician clothes, taking pleasure in his life with Dido, and even supervising work on the building of Carthage.

Jupiter himself sent Mercury to remind Aeneas forcibly of his duty to his son and his descendants. From that moment Aeneas allowed himself to be ruled only by his destiny. He determined to leave Carthage, keeping the news from Dido until the last moment. When she discovered the truth, Dido pleaded passionately with him to stay, but he was resolute. In a fury of rejection, she called upon her people to ensure that they would in future make no pact with Aeneas's people, but 'contend in war, themselves and all the children of their children', thus foretelling the wars between Rome and Carthage. She had a pyre made of everything Aeneas had abandoned.

Then she mounted it and plunged a knife into her breast. Aeneas's ships left Carthage in the tragic glow from Dido's funeral pyre.

The Trojans sailed once again to Sicily, where they commemorated the anniversary of the death of Anchises with funeral games. While the games were in progress, Juno incited the women to set fire to four of the ships in an attempt to bring an end to their weary journeying. Aeneas therefore left some of the older, weaker travellers with a leader to stay and settle in Sicily. Venus pleaded with Neptune to allow the travellers to continue unmolested by Juno, and he agreed, save that one of the crew must die as a token sacrifice. Somnus, Sleep, therefore overcame the helmsman Palinurus, who fell from the ship and drowned.

At last, Aeneas landed in Italy and found the

(Bardo Museum, Tunis) The journey of Aeneas from Troy to the western coast of Italy as described in the Aeneid *deliberately evokes echoes of the journey of the Greek hero Odysseus (Latin Ulysses) from Troy to his home in Ithaca as described by Homer in the* Odyssey. *This Roman mosaic shows Ulysses tied to the mast as he passes the Sirens in order not to be lured by them on the rocks. Mosaic from Dougga.*

*The view from the site of ancient
Carthage today: the Bay of Tunis in
the evening.*

Sibyl at Cumae, as he had been advised. Once again, Virgil is being tactful in setting one of Aeneas's most important experiences in a Greek colony, at a place sacred to Apollo, the god whose cult Augustus had exalted in Rome as a sign of reconciliation between Greece and Rome. The Sibyl told Aeneas that he might enter the Underworld only by carrying with him a golden bough from a certain tree sacred to Juno. His mother, Venus, then sent two doves to direct him to the tree.

Aeneas crossed the river to the Underworld, almost sinking Charon's ferry with his living weight. Once there, he encountered Dido and pleaded for her forgiveness, but she turned from him to the shade of her first husband, to whose love she was restored. Aeneas's most important meeting, however, was with the spirit of his father, Anchises, who explained the Underworld to him in an interesting mixture of philosophies popular in Virgil's day. He then showed him his future wife, Lavinia, and his descendants, who would be future kings of the Latin city of Alba Longa (now Castel Gandolfo). He foretold the founding of Rome by Romulus and then showed Aeneas future Roman rulers, culminating in Augustus, its second founder, 'who shall bring once again an Age of Gold to Latium' and who would extend his power throughout the earth. After this,

Anchises listed the kings of Rome who would rule between its foundation and the Republic, showing the important things each would do. He mentioned a number of great Roman families, and after describing the heroic actions of future Roman generals, said:

'Roman, remember by your strength to rule
Earth's people – for your arts are to be these:
To pacify, to impose the rule of law,
To spare the conquered, battle down the proud.'

Anchises then spoke to Aeneas of wars he would have to fight in the future and of what he must do, then escorted him and the Sibyl to the Ivory Gate, through which they re-entered the world.

Aeneas rejoined his small fleet and they rowed safely past the island of the sorceress, Circe, disturbed by the howls and roars of the chained beasts who had been men before they drank her magic potions. In the calm dawn, they came at last to the mouth of the river Tiber. After pulling the ships onto a tree-lined shore, the company made a feast, piling wild fruit on to the hard wheaten crusts they used as plates. Hunger drove them to eat the crusts as well, at which young Ascanius observed that they had even eaten their plates. Aeneas recognized this as the prophecy he had been given and blessed the land, which he realized was meant as their new home and fatherland.

Aeneas then made an embassy to the local king, Latinus, to ask for a strip of coastal land. Latinus, the old and peace-loving king of Laurentum, welcomed him warmly. He was, says Virgil, the son of Faunus and a Laurentine nymph, and therefore descended from Saturn (Greek Kronos), whose rule in those parts had been a golden age. Here Virgil can be seen using an artificially created genealogy that has turned early Italian deities into the king and queen of a Latin tribe. Latinus had no sons to follow him, but he had a daughter. Portents and oracles had clustered about her that suggested she would bring renown to her people, but also war; it was said that she should marry a man from abroad, a stranger. From that marriage rulers of a great empire would spring.

When Latinus met Aeneas, he recognized him as the stranger his daughter should marry. A local prince, Turnus of the Rutulian tribe, had already claimed Lavinia, however, and Lavinia's mother was sympathetic to his claim. Herein lay the seeds of discord. Juno sent Allecto, a Fury, to poison the minds of the Queen and Turnus and to inflame their anger against Aeneas. Turnus incited his supporters to join him, and Latinus was no longer able to keep the peace when Ascanius, the son of Aeneas, unknowingly influenced by Juno, killed a pet stag that was cherished by the daughter of Turnus's herdsman.

Her brothers, together with other herdsmen and farmers all armed themselves for war. Thirteen Italian chieftains joined Turnus against Aeneas, including Mezentius, former king of Caere in Etruria, who had been exiled for his outrageous acts of cruelty. Tarchon, the reigning king of Etruria, joined Aeneas because he had learned it was the only way to rid himself of Mezentius; other Etruscans also joined Aeneas.

While these events were taking shape, Aeneas,

(Paestum Museum) The upper section of this Lucanian funerary stele from Paestum in southern Italy shows the spirit of the deceased entering the ferryboat of Charon in order to cross the River Styx and enter the Underworld.

(Louvre Museum, Paris) Statue of the River Tiber as a god; he can be identified by the wolf that nurses Romulus and Remus, the founders of Rome. It shows the extent to which the spirits of place were anthropomorphized in the later period. Virgil makes this god appear physically to Aeneas, although in early Rome he would have been perceived simply as the spirit of the river.

stantly at war with the Latins. These genealogies are again transparently Greek, invented on the basis of a mistaken link between the words Pallas and Palatine.

On the next day Aeneas prayed to the river god for confirmation, and saw the white sow and her litter lying on a grassy bank. After dedicating the animals to Juno, the Trojans rowed upstream to Pallanteum, which was built on the Palatine Hill that later became the earliest part of the city of Rome. It was, as yet, 'a meagre town'.

Evander's conversation with Aeneas is a most significant part of the poem. He explains that, although he is Greek and Aeneas Trojan, they share a common ancestor in the Giant Atlas, who holds the heavens on his shoulders. In this way, Aeneas can be seen to share in the Greek heritage, in spite of having been a Trojan enemy.

Evander and his people were celebrating their annual festival dedicated to Hercules, and he tells Aeneas how Hercules had come to that spot in earlier days and killed the monster Cacus, who lived in a cave there. The cult of Hercules, who was the Roman version of the Greek hero Heracles, was widespread in the western Mediterranean, where he was seen as a god rather than as a hero who had been assumed into the Olympian pantheon at the end of his life, which is how he appears in Greek myths. Virgil here draws a parallel between heroic qualities of Hercules in driving evil forces from the land and Aeneas's own potential for doing so.

Evander explains that the golden age of Saturn once reigned in that land and that he himself had come there in exile, urged by his mother, the nymph Carmentis, and through her by Apollo. From the Palatine Hill, he shows Aeneas some of the places that were to become significant in later Rome. In this way Virgil uses invented myths to account for and give importance to names that were used but not fully understood in his own day. Among these are: the Carmental gate, named after Evander's mother; the wood where Romulus would seek refuge; the Lupercal grotto; the Tarpeian Hill; the rock on which the Capitol would be built, and the Janiculum, founded by the god Janus. The reader suspects a contemporary joke when Virgil makes Aeneas hear cattle lowing 'in what is now Rome's Forum and her fashionable quarter, Carinae'. With great generosity, Evander then gave his son Pallas to Aeneas as a companion in war.

Aeneas left Pallanteum at the head of his army. When they paused, Venus presented him with some powerfully protective armour that she had persuaded her husband, Vulcan (Greek Hephaestus), the smith and fire-god to make. The shield was particularly

'heartsick at the woe of war' rested by the river Tiber. The god of the river raised his head from the water and urged Aeneas to stay in that land, promising him that the next day he should see the white sow and her piglets, as had been prophesied. Roman readers would have recognized in the white sow an ancient portent signifying the foundation of Alba Longa, since the word for white in Latin is *alba*. The river god also urged Aeneas to search out an Arcadian tribe, that is a tribe of colonists from Arcadia in Greece, who were descended from a forebear called Pallas, and had founded a town called Pallanteum, under King Evander. They were con-

remarkable because on it the god, with his fore-knowledge, had wrought the future story of Italy. By describing the details of the shield, the poet is able to summarize the traditional history of Rome – its foundation by Romulus; the threats of Porsenna and others and the heroic response of people like Horatius and Manlius; and, closer to his own age, Cato's law-giving and the sea-battle of Actium, led by Augustus Caesar, from whose 'blessed brow twin flames gush upward'. The shield also shows Augustus's triumph following Actium, in which many conquered races from Africa to the Rhine, speaking varied languages, passed 'in long procession'.

War now breaks out and much of the rest of the poem recounts the epic contests between the warriors fighting on the sides of either Aeneas or Turnus. Young Ascanius has his moment of heroism, after which he is addressed by Apollo, who calls him, significantly, by his other name of Iulus. Apollo also calls him 'son of gods and sire of gods to come', a reference to the deification of Julius Caesar and successive emperors, which will be discussed later.

On one occasion Turnus describes himself as a 'new Achilles', a reference to the great Greek hero who fought the Trojans, and this is typical of the heroism Virgil allows to the enemy of Aeneas. Turnus was, after all, Italian and thus, in a historic sense, engaged in a civil war with Aeneas. He was not an enemy from outside, and Virgil must give credit to the bravery of the warring tribes of Italy and suggest how they became united under Rome. Yet he sees the pity of it.

Jupiter is distressed by the conflict. 'The time for war will come,' he says, and predicts the future savagery of Carthage in its attack on Roman towns. In the struggle between Juno and Venus, Jupiter refuses to take sides, and leaves the outcome to Fate.

Aeneas is overcome with guilt when Turnus kills Pallas, the young son of his ally Evander, but he himself kills the hated Etruscan, Mezentius. Interestingly, Aeneas has an ally in another Etruscan, Tarchon, who is clearly a good man. Thus Virgil shows two sides to the Etruscan story in Italy.

Aeneas tries in vain to make peace and challenges Turnus to single combat as a way of settling their differences and putting an end to the killing of so many innocent people, but Turnus refuses. Seeing the carnage, Jupiter finally forbids Juno to go any

Detail from the Ara Pacis Augustae, *or Altar of Augustan Peace, in Rome. Aeneas, with his cloak drawn over his head in the manner of a priest, offers a sacrifice, probably the one made at Lanuvium on his arrival in Italy. It echoes a figure of Augustus similarly offering sacrifice on another panel of the altar.*

further in stirring up men to war. In return, she pleads that once Aeneas and Lavinia are married Latin people will not have to become Trojans in any way. She pleads:

'Let Latium be

Let there be Alban kings for generations,

And let Italian valour be the strength

Of Rome in after times.'

In other worlds Italian toughness and vigour will help to make Rome great in the future. Jupiter agrees, saying that no nation on earth will honour her so faithfully, and Juno withdraws from the scene.

The final act of the poem is the single combat between Aeneas and Turnus, reminding us of that between Achilles and Hector in the *Iliad*. At the last, when Turnus is at Aeneas's mercy and pleads for his life, Aeneas pauses, but then sees that Turnus is wearing the sword belt he had taken from young Pallas after he killed him. At this, anger blazes in Aeneas, and he kills Turnus on behalf of Pallas. The poem ends as the soul of Turnus passes to the shades.

The *Aeneid* demonstrates the human cost of achieving power, as well as its glory. Details throughout the poem reveal Virgil's sensitivity to the effect of power on humble, individual lives. Yet the poem clearly declares that Roman domination of the world was foretold by the gods, and that Roman power will impose peace and civilization upon those who come within its orbit. It takes up a number of strands in Rome's history – Etruscan, Italian, Greek, Sicilian – and tries to give value to each and to reconcile them. The poem became extremely popular and extremely influential, and ultimately the Roman people accepted their Trojan origin as part of their own myth.

ABOVE
(Florence Archaeological Museum)
Aeneas fought one Etruscan warrior but was supported by another. This warrior is painted on a Etruscan sarcophagus of the 4th century BC.

LEFT
The view from the Palatine Hill today. In the foreground are the remains of the Roman Forum, the great central meeting place of Rome, where Virgil's Aeneas saw cattle grazing long before the city existed.

CHAPTER THREE
MYTHS OF ROME (2): THE FOUNDATION OF ROME AND THE EARLY KINGS

The story of Romulus and Remus, to which Virgil refers, had been told in various versions for several centuries by his period, and illustrates the complex growth of a foundation myth. It is another of the national legends that formed part of the myth of Rome and, like the story of Aeneas, probably owed its importance to the concentration on the family and the state in Roman religion and to a veneration of ancestors that verged on ancestor-worship.

By the fifth century BC, Greek writers were using the name Rhomos for the founder of the city who also gave his name to it; the Italians, however, used the term Romulus, meaning 'of Rome'; hence possibly the distinction into two separate men, Latin Romulus and Greek Rhomos, corrupted to Remus in Latin. In fact the origin of the names is probably much more complicated than that, as one or both of the twins occur in a number of written stories from the fourth century BC, stories that had probably been told orally before that.

It will be seen that their story has many characteristics of early myths and folk-tales from other traditions: jealousy between brothers leading to fratricide, the fathering of children on a mortal woman by a god – a frequent feat of the Greek gods, but not of early Italian deities – children abandoned in a floating cradle, the suckling of infants by an animal and the restoration of sons to their family. The story was written down in the third century by Fabius Pictor, apparently from a Greek original, and then frequently repeated in various versions in the first century

BC. It was probably largely a Greek invention overlaying what may have been a traditional story.

The version that became accepted by the Romans of the Empire was the one written by Livy in the period of Augustus. Livy, or Titus Livius, who was born at Padua in about 60 BC, devoted his life to writing his *History of Rome* in 142 books, of which 35 survive. It soon became regarded as authoritative by his contemporaries, although what strikes us now is the way in which he dramatizes events, and views them through the eyes of a moralist, rather as a novelist might do today.

He places the brothers Romulus and Remus in the line of Alban kings descended from the son of Aeneas that was invented in order to fill in the time gap between Aeneas's departure from Troy, which was thought to have been in about 1100 BC, and the founding of Rome, thought to have been in 753 BC. In the tradition of Roman historians, he uses the ancient events he describes to account for and dignify the contemporary topography of his own Rome. It was possibly this that helped to give his version authenticity for his first readers who saw daily the places he described.

Livy lists a selection of the kings of Alba until he arrives at the brothers Numitor and Amulius. The younger of these, Amulius, drove Numitor from the throne, murdered his male children and made Numitor's daughter, Rhea Silvia, a Vestal Virgin so that she would have no children to threaten his reign. His plans promised to come to nothing when Rhea Silvia was raped by the god Mars, as she claimed, and gave birth to twin sons. Amulius imprisoned her and condemned the children, Romulus and Remus, to drowning in the river.

The river had flooded and the men entrusted with the drowning carelessly left the children in a basket in shallow flood water near the Ruminal fig-tree, a tree that grew in Rome in Livy's day and that he suggests once took its name from Romulus. Other versions of the story suggest that *ruma* or *rumis* was an early Latin word for breast, and as Rumina was the goddess of nursing mothers and the fig tree oozes a milky juice that was thought of as a fertility charm, this was an appropriate place for the twins to be nourished.

The surrounding country was still quite wild, and a she-wolf, coming to the river to drink, heard the children cry and offered them her teats to suck. Faustulus, the king's herdsman, happened to pass and saw her gently licking the children with her tongue. He took them home to his wife, Larentia, who nursed the children and brought them up. Livy adds that some people think the origin of this story was that Larentia was a common prostitute, who was called 'Lupa', or Wolf, by the other shepherds. He also links the site with the ancient Roman festival, the Lupercalia, that was still celebrated with unusual rites in Livy's life-time, but whose origins had become obscure.

(Capitoline Museums, Rome) This famous she-wolf of Rome is thought to be an Etruscan bronze of the late 6th or early 5th century BC, which originally stood on the Capitol. The twins, Romulus and Remus, are not part of the original composition, however, but were added in the early 16th century.

RIGHT
In this Etruscan bronze a seated augur closely observes a flight of birds to see what they portend.

TOP RIGHT
This relief in the Roman Forum illustrates the seizing of marriageable Sabine women by young Romans in need of wives.

RIGHT
In this relief the boundaries, or sacred furrows, of a new city are ceremonially ploughed. This custom originated with the Etruscans whose Books of Ritual insisted that each city had to be surrounded by a pomerium, or sacred boundary, to safeguard the population.

He does not refer the Lupercalia to the wolf that nourished Romulus and Remus, however, but to an annual festival in honour of Pan Lyceas, or 'wolfish Pan', a Greek minor deity, whose worship, said Greek story-tellers, had been instituted on the Palatine Hill by Evander, the Arcadian ruler who had welcomed Aeneas there many years earlier. Scholars now suggest that the names of the herdsman and his wife, Faustulus and Larentia, were actually those of local rural deities, and that Greek writers before Livy had turned them into people in a way that was fashionable among writers at the time.

One day, when the Festival of the Lupercalia was in progress, some brigands arrived on the scene, angry because Romulus and Remus, who were now shepherds, had been seizing from them goods they had stolen and sharing them out with the other shepherds. They attacked the twins and succeeded in capturing Remus and handing him over to king Amulius. Remus was charged with stealing from Numitor's land and was therefore passed to

him for punishment.

The truth about the twins' identity was then revealed and, once Remus had been released by his newly-discovered grandfather, the two young men attacked and killed the usurper, Amulius. Numitor summoned his subjects, confessed the whole story and assumed responsibility for the murder of his brother. Romulus and Remus supported him, and he was established once more as King.

Romulus and Remus then determined to found a new settlement on the spot by the Tiber where they had been both abandoned and nourished, and they were encouraged to do so by the fact that Alba was by now over-populated. Sadly, they succumbed to jealousy and ambition, just as their uncle had done before them. As twins, neither could assume authority, so they asked the gods of the countryside to send omens to determine which of them should govern and give his name to the new town. Romulus went to the Palatine Hill and Remus to the Aventine to observe the omens or auguries.

Remus was the first to see a sign – six vultures, but double that number of birds then appeared to Romulus. Supporters of both men claimed that the evidence of the omens favoured their side and in the affray that followed Remus was killed. A more common explanation of that death is, however, says Livy, that Remus taunted his brother by jumping over the half-built walls of his new settlement, at which the enraged Romulus killed him, threatening to do the same to anyone who leapt over his battlements.

It was in this fratricide that some Romans saw the seeds of the civil wars of the first century. The threat about the battlements, in fact, encapsulated the seriousness with which the Romans treated the sanctity of their *pomerium*, or boundary. This had originally been a sacred area, a clear, ploughed strip on both sides of the boundary of any town, on which nothing might be built and which no unauthorized person might cross.

Romulus fortified the Palatine Hill and sacrificed to the gods. Following Evander's example, he worshipped Hercules in the Greek fashion, that is, presumably, bare-headed. He gave laws to his subjects and created a hundred senators, or fathers of the city, *patres*, whose descendants became the patricians, the aristocrats of Rome, as opposed to the plebeians or common people.

He then created a sanctuary for fugitives in order to help increase the population of his new city. This has been seen as a traditional explanation for the later mixture of people who lived in the city. There were, however, not enough women to ensure the future of the city and requests to other cities for female immigrants were scornfully refused.

The problem was solved by a desperate measure. Romulus invited the surrounding tribes, including the Sabines, to the great annual festival of the Consualia, held in honour of Neptune. First, his people courteously showed their visitors, who had brought their sons and daughters with them, round the new city. Immediately the festival began, however, the marriageable men of Rome ran through the crowds and seized all the marriageable daughters who had come with their parents. Certain senators ensured that particularly desirable young women were seized on their behalf. The festival broke up in panic, and the girls' angry parents escaped, lamenting the deception.

Romulus reassured the terrified young women in turn, telling them that they would be honoured as married women and, eventually, mothers, sharing the privileges of the community. The men assured their chosen wives that their action had been

The god Janus – one of the earliest gods of Rome. He was originally the god of doorways and thus came to be represented with two heads, one looking forward and one back. He was often shown on bronze coins, like this one of the Republican period, because he was thought to have invented money.

prompted by love, and the women gradually accepted their husbands and settled down happily enough to motherhood.

The neighbouring communities began a series of attacks on Rome and were beaten back until the Sabines, under their king Titus Tatius, entered Rome through the treachery of a young Roman woman, Tarpeia, the daughter of the commander of the Roman citadel. She was bribed by Tatius to admit some of his soldiers into the citadel. Once inside, the soldiers crushed her to death under their shields; some say this was her punishment because she had asked, as her price, 'what they had on their shield arms'. By this she had meant their rings and gold bracelets, but they chose to interpret it as their shields. Tarpeia's name was probably once that of an ancient local goddess, or it might have been the Sabine form of the Etruscan name Tarquinia, but Livy's story about her gives sinister significance to the Tarpeian Rock on the Capitoline Hill, from which criminals were once thrown to their death.

The Romans and Sabines fought together on the marshy ground between the Palatine and Capitoline Hills, and it seemed that the Sabine hero, Mettus Curtius, might sink into the swamp. The situation was saved when the Sabine women, fearless of danger, threw themselves between the armies. They begged their fathers and brothers to stop fighting their husbands, who were now also the fathers of

their children. They cried that they would rather be killed themselves than be widowed or orphaned. Silence fell and not a man moved. Peace was concluded and the two states were united under a single government, with Rome as the seat of power. The Romans, as a gesture to the Sabines says Livy, began to call themselves Quirites, after the Sabine town of Cures. The marsh in which Curtius had almost drowned was renamed Lacus Curtius.

In telling this story, Livy has accounted for a fact of history, which was that the Romans were descended not simply from a Latin community but also from Sabine communities on surrounding hills that were later incorporated into the city. It seems likely that the story of the rape of the Sabine women may have developed to account for a noticeable Sabine element in the population of Rome, and also in an attempt to explain an obscure but lasting feature of the Roman marriage ceremony, which is still familiar to anthropologists as 'marriage by capture'. When, after the wedding feast, the bride was led to the bridegroom's house she was dragged away from her mother's arms in a show of force by the bridegroom.

Romulus continued a successful reign, and was particularly loved by the commons and the army. One day, while he was reviewing his troops on the Campus Martius, a violent storm broke. A thick cloud enveloped him, and from that moment he was never seen again. When the soldiers saw the empty throne and realized Romulus had been carried up to the heavens by a whirlwind they proclaimed him a divinity, hailing him as a god and son of the god Mars. Livy nods to a story that the senate had torn him to pieces, but dismisses it.

The matter was settled later by a wise man, Julius Proculus, who addressed the Assembly one day, telling them that Romulus had descended to him from heaven at dawn and told him to tell the Romans that 'by heaven's will my Rome shall be capital of the world', that they should learn to be soldiers and teach their children that no power on earth could stand against Roman arms. Romulus had then been taken up again into the sky.

This incident is significant. It reflects the experience of the great hero Hercules, who was lifted up to heaven from his funeral pyre and deified. It places Romulus and therefore other Roman rulers in that tradition, and it foreshadows events in Livy's own day: the first moves towards the deification of the Emperors of Rome, about which more will be said later. The story of deification also helps to explain how Romulus became assimilated to the very early Roman god, Quirinus, who was the third of the

Roman triad of great gods, with Jupiter and Mars. Quirinus was probably originally a Sabine god of war, and possibly of agriculture, and his name may be associated with the Sabine town, Cures, or with the Sabine word for lance, *curis*.

In common with other historians of his age, Livy accounts for the period from the traditional foundation of Rome in 753 BC to the beginning of the Republic in 509 BC with rule by seven kings. He shows how the population of the city increased by means of gradual victories over surrounding cities and the absorption of their population into Rome. It is thought that there may be some historical truth in his detail, but the pattern of kingship he presents is sufficiently schematic to cast doubt on much of what he says.

A warlike king is usually succeeded by one dedicated to social administration or the construction of buildings and temples, and a good Etruscan king is followed by an equally bad one. It seems likely that elements of folk-lore, legend, fact, cult and oral tradition had been converted into a myth intended to stress the Latin origins, valour and great virtues of the Roman people.

NUMA POMPILIUS was the successor to Romulus; he was a Sabine from Cures and thus neatly accounts for the amalgamation of the two peoples. Unlike Romulus, he was not a man of war, but was deeply learned in the laws of god and man. Characters like him are often found in legend or folklore as inventors of customs and ceremonies that seem to later generations ancient but inexplicable. He gave the city a 'second beginning', on a solid basis of law and religious observance. He instituted the Temple of Janus, an important Roman monument, whose doors were left open in time of war so that the god could come to the help of the Romans, but kept closed in time of peace.

It is easy to see in Numa the deliberate creation of a figure who inspired the essentially Roman virtues admired by men like Augustus, and who could be credited with the introduction of a number of Rome's major religious and administrative practices that must have actually grown up over the centuries. Numa was troubled by the behaviour of the Romans in his day, so he decided to inspire them with 'fear of the gods'. To this end, he invented the fiction that he met each night with the goddess Egeria who gave him the authority to establish certain religious rites and priesthoods.

His story includes one piece of possibly genuine folklore. When Numa summoned the god Jupiter in order to discover the expiatory ritual to adopt when something was struck by lightening, Jupiter listed the materials to be used in the sacrifice. He demanded a head, 'of garlic', said Numa; 'human...' 'hair', interrupted Numa, and 'the life...' 'of a sprat', said Numa. Because he was amused, Jupiter agreed to the garlic, hair and small fish, which were, in fact, the puzzling materials used in the rite.

Numa established a Calendar of twelve lunar months with intercalary months to provide adjustment to the full cycle. Then he fixed the 'lawful' and 'unlawful' days on which men might or might not transact business, an important feature of Roman life that we shall look at later.

He established virgin priestesses for the cult of Vesta, which he imported from Alba. Among the priesthoods he established were the twelve Salii, or dancing priests, whose annual ritual, in which they danced through Rome chanting words no one could any longer understand, survived in Livy's day. He ensured that no natural religious rite should be neglected and that foreign rites should be properly adopted, a feature of religious life that was to be rather more important in later years when Rome had contact with many other countries. He reigned for forty-three peaceful years, and his reign acted as a balance to the warlike reign of Romulus.

TULLUS HOSTILIUS, the next king, was a soldier and conducted a bitter civil war with Alba, whose citizens were of the same descent as the Romans. During the war two families made a typically Roman sacrificial gesture in which they put loyalty to the state before their own interest, and thus they serve as one of a number of mythological examples to later Romans. A set of triplets from each side, the Horatii from Rome and the Curatii from Alba, fought each other to decide the outcome of the war. The three Curatii killed two of the Horatii fairly quickly, then the third of the Horatii ran off so that the Curatii were forced to follow him. As they reached him, separately and exhausted, he succeeded in killing each in turn. Horatius returned in triumph to Rome, carrying the armour of the Curatii. When the sister of Horatius, who had been married to one of the Curatii brothers, saw her husband's cloak across her brother's shoulders, she wept for her dead husband. Horatius instantly stabbed his sister for showing her love, saying 'so perish all Roman women who mourn for an enemy.'

Although Horatius was tried for his horrifying deed, his father defended him, saying his daughter had deserved her death. The young man was acquitted, but his father had to perform certain expiatory ceremonies, which then became traditional in the Horatian family. Horatius had to pass under a beam in the roadway, as though under a yoke of submis-

Pavement mosaic at Ostia Antica, the port of ancient Rome, showing a lighthouse and two ships. 2nd-3rd century AD.

sion; the timber, says Livy, is still to be seen, having been replaced from time to time, and is known as the Sister's Beam. In this story, the family pride of the Horatii is celebrated and a respectably antiquarian explanation given for the beam across the road.

Tullus Hostilius destroyed Alba completely, and took its people into Rome, thus doubling the size of the city and increasing the number of families of senatorial rank by the admission of some of the Alban nobility. He built the Senate House for their deliberations, and Livy points out, accurately, that the building had been known until recently as the Curia Hostilia. Tullus Hostilius also fought the Sabines and defeated them. A number of omens, such as a shower of stones on the Alban Mount, warned that the Alban gods should not remain neglected in their deserted temples. When plague broke out in Rome, the king became subject to superstition and, while he was engaged one day in performing secret, and apparently incorrect, expiatory rites to Jupiter, his palace was struck by lightning and he burned to death.

ANCUS MARCIUS, the next king, oversaw a return to religion. He was both soldier and administrator. Under him, ceremonials were established for the formal declaration of 'just wars' after consulta-

tion with the gods and the elders of the city. He also extended the city, built a prison, made better defences and founded the port of Ostia at the mouth of the Tiber, so that Rome could more easily conduct its maritime trade.

LUCIUS TARQUINIUS PRISCUS (Tarquin the First) was a particularly interesting successor to the kingship. He was not a Roman but was born in Tarquinii in Etruria, and was actually an alien, being the son of a Greek immigrant called Demaratus, a noble who had settled in Etruria after leaving Corinth for political reasons. Since Livy places the first Tarquin's reign at the end of the seventh century, there may be some truth in the story of his father's origin. Corinth was ruled by autocrats at that period, and archaeological evidence shows that unusually large amounts of Corinthian pottery were being used in Etruria then.

Before he became king, Tarquinius Priscus was known as Lucumo, which scholars say is simply an Etruscan word for 'lord'. He was a poor but ambitious young man, and his wife, Tanaquil, who was equally ambitious, urged him to try his fortune in Rome. When they arrived there, an eagle swooped down and snatched off his cap; having taken it high into the sky, the bird swooped down again and replaced the cap on Lucumo's head. Tanaquil, reading the omen in the practised manner of an Etruscan, saw this as a sign of greatness to come.

Lucumo courted popularity and when the time came for the choice to be made of a successor to the throne, he ensured that the sons of the previous king, Ancus, were away from Rome. He then secured the vote by a popular majority. He was a man of good ability, but also a schemer, so he added a hundred new members to the Senate, drawing them from the 'lesser men', and knowing that they would support him.

Archaeology suggests that some civic building began in Rome in this period, and it is interesting that the first Tarquin king is credited with building the Circus Maximus, in which he instituted games on Etruscan lines, and with improving the Forum, along with a number of other civic undertakings. He also extended Rome's power by taking the city of Collatia from the Sabines and subduing some of the Latin tribes.

SERVIUS TULLIUS, who succeeded Tarquin, seems to be a mythical figure and may for once have some basis in a genuinely traditional story. Servius came to the attention of Tanaquil, the queen, while her husband Tarquin was still alive. One night, as Servius slept, flames were observed to play harmlessly about his head. Tanaquil felt that he was destined to be great and brought him up as a prince. A different tradition identified him with an adventurous Etruscan hero called Mastarna; in either case he was clearly someone exceptional.

Servius Tullius was said to have been a slave, but Livy cannot accept that, guessing that his mother must have been a prisoner of war. There may be something of a folk-lore element in the story, since

The remains of Roman warehouses in the port of Ostia Antica.

the fourth century BC was a period during which the plebeians, or commons, were agitating for more power in the essentially undemocratic, aristocratic system of government in Rome and his name is a Latin one that would have been used only by plebeian families.

When king Tarquin was murdered by the sons of the former king, Ancus, who had never reconciled themselves to his kingship, Servius substituted for him, at first pretending that the king had merely been wounded. By that time he had become sufficiently popular to be elected king when Tarquin's death was officially announced.

Servius re-organized society, and introduced the census, an invaluable instrument of rule that survived in Rome. He extended the city boundary, taking in two more hills, the Quirinal and the Viminal. One of his most significant acts was to encourage the building of a temple of Diana in Rome as a joint enterprise by the united Latin people; it was a direct attempt to emulate the way in which a combination of Asian people had come together to build a temple of Diana at Ephesus. The mutual venture by the Latin people signified that they had ceased to fight each other, and that Rome was their capital city.

One man from the Sabine people wanted to dispute this notion, however, and saw a chance to do so. On a Sabine farm there was a heifer of such astonishing size and beauty that it seemed to have an almost sacred quality; indeed prophecies had been made that imperial power would belong to the nation whose citizens sacrificed it to Diana. The Roman priest of the new temple of Diana had heard of this prophecy and recognized the heifer when the Sabine brought it to the temple to sacrifice it. The priest asked the man what he could be thinking of to sacrifice the beast without first purifying himself in the living water of the Tiber. While the Sabine went off to suitably cleanse himself, the priest sacrificed the heifer himself, thus confirming Rome's powerful position.

Servius was the last good king; he actually intended to abdicate in favour of a republic but was prevented from doing so by being cruelly murdered by assassins hired by his son-in-law, another Tarquin.

TARQUINIUS SUPERBUS, Tarquin the Proud, who ruled for twenty-five years was a violent usurper who took power without being elected by the people or sanctioned by the Senate. He was an autocrat, ruling without consultation and treating the Latin leaders with contempt. He was, however, a successful soldier and strategist. He conquered the town of Gabii by a ruse. His son, Sextus, went to Gabii, pretending to have fled from the harshness of his father, but in fact he spent his time there gathering friends, reputation and information. When Sextus felt he had the town in his pocket he sent a messenger to his father to ask him what to do next. Tarquinius Superbus walked with the messenger in his garden and, when pressed for an answer, said nothing but knocked the heads off tall-growing poppies with his stick. The puzzled messenger reported this action to Sextus, who understood the silent message and responded by getting rid of all the prominent men in Gabii so that the town fell into Tarquin's hands.

In Rome, Tarquin began to build the temple of Jupiter on the Capitoline. He also set men to work on the Cloaca Maxima, the Great Sewer of Rome. A number of portents began to disturb his reign. When a snake slid out from a crack in a wooden pillar in the palace, Tarquin sent two of his sons, Titus and Arruns, to the oracle at Delphi in Greece. They took with them Lucius Junius Brutus, the king's nephew.

Brutus had learned to feign stupidity when he was with the brothers in order not to appear as a threat to their succession to the throne, and so be killed. Both brothers were intensely ambitious and, after they had put Tarquin's questions to the oracle, they asked one of their own: which of them would be the next king of Rome? The answer came: 'He who shall first kiss his mother shall hold supreme authority in Rome.'

While Titus and Arruns were drawing lots for the privilege of being the first to get back to their mother Brutus pretended to trip. He fell on his face and kissed the earth – the mother of all living things.

Once back in Rome the brothers were sent on a long campaign against the town of Ardea. One day while they were drinking with friends in Sextus's quarters, they began to boast about their wives. One of the young men, Collatinus, suggested they should all ride to Rome and see what their wives were doing that evening. The wives of the two young princes were found at a lavish dinner party with friends. In Collatia, however, Lucretia, the beautiful wife of Collatinus, was sitting with her servants spinning, despite the late hour. Collatinus invited his friends to take supper with him and his wife. Sextus, watching Lucretia, determined that she should be his.

A few days later, he returned to Collatia, where he was treated like an honoured guest in Lucretia's house and escorted to a guest chamber. During the night he found his way to Lucretia's room, where he raped her. She struggled and he succeeded only by threatening that if she refused him he would kill her and leave a dead slave beside her to suggest that she

had died as a result of her adultery with a slave.

When he had gone, Lucretia wrote to her father and her husband asking each to come at once with a trusted friend. When her husband arrived with Brutus she confessed to her adultery with Sextus Tarquinius and asked that he should be punished. They swore he should and tried to comfort her, but she could not forgive herself. She plunged a knife into her breast and killed herself for shame. By doing this she became a pattern of the pure and steadfast wife, and her example has been quoted in literature and shown in painting and sculpture from that day to this.

Brutus took the knife and called upon the men to swear vengeance. He revealed his true nature at last and led a rebellion against Tarquinius Superbus and his family. The monarchy came to an end and a republic took its place. Two consuls were elected by popular vote; they were Lucius Junius Brutus and Lucius Tarquinius Collatinus.

The story of king Tarquin and his son was clearly invented to explain the sudden and violent end of the monarchy, and the end of Etruscan power in Rome. There are features of Tarquin's reign, such as the building of the Capitoline temple, that seem to have a basis in fact, but the rape of Lucretia is probably a fable devised to explain what was in fact a fairly common decline in monarchic rule throughout the Latin tribes.

The deposed king went for help to some local kings, in particular to Lars Porsenna of Clusium. Porsenna mounted an attack on Rome, making for the wooden bridge over the Tiber. A heroic Roman, Horatius Cocles, stayed alone on the bridge, fending off the attack, to allow his fellow soldiers to destroy the bridge behind him. Just as the bridge was severed, he leapt into the Tiber and swam to safety. 'Cocles' means one-eyed, and this feat was later associated with the statue of a one-eyed man near the bridge, which was probably, in fact, a statue of the god Vulcan. Nevertheless, the myth provided another source of pride for the Horatian family. The truth was probably that Porsenna actually captured Rome although he stayed there only briefly. Roman history in its more mythical version does not, however, feel the need to acknowledge that uncomfortable fact.

Whatever the truth of the stories of the kings, the violent ending of their rule reflected the horror of kingship felt by republican Romans, and their determination that no king would reign in Rome again. That determination helps to explain the assassination of Julius Caesar at the moment when it seemed he might accept an offer of kingship.

It is now thought that the stories about the Etruscan kings also contain a grain of truth in that the Etruscans were in power in Rome during a period when the city actually expanded in size and importance. Most importantly, these are myths and legends that were told to and repeated by people who were amazed at the speed at which their city had grown in size and power, who valued their traditions and who wanted to find explanations for them and give them respectability and significance by placing them in a recognized historical tradition.

CHAPTER FOUR
DOMESTIC RELIGION AND THE EARLY GODS OF ROME

(National Museum, Naples) A mythological landscape from the walls of the Villa of Agrippa near Pompeii that is typical of fashionable painting there of the mid-1st century AD. While it is derived from Hellenistic art, it shows the continuing Roman feeling for the spirit of landscape.

It is, of course, impossible now to recover accurately the earliest gods of the Roman people. Our information about them comes chiefly from educated men looking back at the past from a distance of several centuries in an attempt to find the origin of ancient cult traditions. Such information as we have suggests very strongly that the instinctive religion of the early Romans was a kind of animism, in which many things, both natural and man-made, were felt to be operated and informed by the divine spirit that inhabited them. These spirits were known as *numina*, and were probably not originally differentiated as individual gods. Perhaps we can most easily envisage them now in our own reaction to some tree, rock, forest or river-meadow that seems to have a special, almost sacred quality, and in our reaction to objects that we want to be able to use in as trouble-free a manner as possible.

Surviving literature and inscriptions carved in stone suggest that the Romans felt that the gods set in motion all the important activities of their world, and that different activities were the responsibility of specific gods who existed simply to perform them and nothing else. Once people had named the gods, they added adjectives to the names to indicate precise functions. Thus Janus, the god who had power over doors, was known as Janus Patulcius when he opened them and Janus Clusivius when he closed them.

These gods had names but they did not, like the Greek gods, have personalities, personal histories or myths. They simply had functions. On one often-

(British Museum, London) A bronze lar, *a spirit who watched over the household, the family and its lands. These early spirits continued to be honoured in the home for many centuries, as is shown by this one dating from the 1st-2nd century AD.*

quoted occasion, as late as the second century AD, when priests removed a fig-tree from a shrine, it is recorded that they invoked three gods to help them: Adolenda, or 'Burner', Commolenda, or 'Smasher', and Deferunda, or 'Carrier Away', thus calling upon divine backing for each part of the process.

Such customs were likely to survive among a conservative priesthood, of course, but it seems likely that the same kind of consciousness of the divine forces behind everyday activities remained with the average Roman for a very long time. Educated men later turned for spiritual satisfaction to the Greek gods, to philosophy or to the idea of one divine spirit, but even the sophisticated poet Ovid could still say of a cluster of oak trees that anyone seeing it would say 'a deity lives there'.

Man's relationship with the gods was functional, almost contractual; it was his duty to recognize their help and acknowledge it when things went well, or to find out what the gods wanted and put it right when things went badly. Religion was not a question of belief but of behaviour, and that is why it now looks to us like superstition.

The familiar, domestic gods were recognized particularly in three areas of life: the household, the agricultural year, and those important moments in life we now know as rites of passage, such as birth, the onset of puberty, marriage and death. The Romans, like most people who are primarily agriculturalists or small traders, centred their lives on the family and household. Wealthier households would include servants and slaves. The head of the household, the father or *pater familias*, was responsible for its continuity and, in the early period, also had the power of life and death over its members. He had his own Genius, or guardian spirit, sometimes represented visually as a snake, and was responsible for maintaining the household's relationship with the divinities that surrounded them. These included such precise functionaries as Cardea, the goddess of door hinges, Forculus, the god of doors, Janus, the god of doorways, and Limentinus, the god of the threshold.

Chief among the household gods were the Penates and the Lares. The Penates were the divinities of the penus or store-cupboard. They were not personalized and no one even knew how many of them there were, except that they were plural. They were the gods of the home in a very intimate way, the ones who ensured a supply of food and to whom the family made small offerings at the main meal every day. They would have been among the gods Aeneas carried with him from Troy because they would have represented home. They were worshipped at the hearth, which was the home of the goddess Vesta

42

who, like her Greek equivalent, Hestia, was so ancient that she never acquired a personality.

The other household gods were the Lares, who were often spoken of in the plural, although there was a singular spirit called a Lar. The Lares cared for the household in general, including its land. They were often identified with the spirits of the ancestors of the family, who were extremely important to the Romans, and they guarded the family as a whole from one generation to the next, patrolling the fields to keep away harmful spirits. Each household would have its lararium, or shrine, a cupboard containing small statuettes representing their Lares, which might also be used as a depository for valuables. The family would make them a monthly offering of cakes, milk or wine in gratitude for their guardianship.

Unusually, the Lares watched over slaves as well as the other members of the household, so slaves celebrated their particular relationship with them at an annual rural festival called the Compitalia, or Laralia. This was held at the *compitum* or point where several properties met, and a shrine would be set up there for each set of Lares, together with a ploughshare. Each free person would be represented by a suspended wooden doll, and each slave by a ball of wool. The festival was imported into the city of Rome by rural immigrants and later came to be celebrated at crossroads in the swarming city by large groups of poor people who actually had by then no rural memories. It frequently gave concern to the authorities.

In the fields, there were even more divine functionaries than there were in the home, with separate, named, gods for the first and second ploughings, the harrowing, sowing, top-dressing and so on. Spiniensis was invoked to help clear a field of thorns and Stercutius to manure it. Robigus, the god of rust, or mildew, was propitiated on 25 April by the sacrifice of a rust-coloured dog. Consus was the god of

Wall-painting from a lararium *or household shrine in the House of the Vetii, Pompeii. The head of the household, the* pater familias*, is shown with his head covered as for a religious ritual, and holds an incense box in one hand. Two* lares *accompany him. The* genius*, or guardian spirit, of the* pater familias *is represented by the snake below. 1st century AD.*

A typical agricultural task of ploughing with an ox is shown in this Roman relief from Nîmes in France.

the granary, and Ops of the wealth of the harvest.

Pales, whose origin is particularly obscure, was possibly once a pair of shepherd-deities, male and female, responsible for keeping flocks safe from disease. This deity continued to be celebrated in later Rome in a festival called the Parilia, held on the Palatine Hill, where Rome originated. It seems likely that by that time the name of the god had become associated with the name of the hill. The celebrations concluded with a great meal in the open air, after which everyone leaped three times through the flames of a bonfire. It had clearly become a festival to celebrate the birth and renewal of the city, rather than having anything to do with flocks of sheep.

Terminus was the stone used to mark property boundaries, and a stone called by that name became a divinity in Rome itself. Each activity had its divinity, and at the edge of the farm, in the woodland, might have lurked the divinities of wilder nature, Faunus or Silvanus.

The rites of passage through life also had their divinities. At birth separate goddesses were responsible for the foetus, the pregnancy, and the birth itself, which was overseen by Juno Lucina. After the birth, there was a ceremony in which evil spirits were driven away with an axe, a stake and a broom, overseen by Intercidona, Pilumnus and Deverra. There were even named spirits who guarded the cra-

dle, induced the first cry, helped with breast-feeding and so on.

In early Rome the patricians and plebeians had different marriage ceremonies. No religious rites were legally required of either group, but among the patricians homage was often made to the gods in a number of ways. The marriage was celebrated at the bride's father's household altar, where the bride and groom shared a cake made of spelt, a kind of wheat, following a sacrifice that had been sprinkled with a gruel made of spelt. On the eve of her wedding day the bride would have made an offering of her dolls to the Lares of her father's household. The marriage ceremony was held in the early morning, but only if the omens were favourable. The bride sought the goodwill of the gods of the threshold of her new home by decorating it with flowers and wool and smearing the door posts and lintels with oil.

Ancestors were very important to the Romans throughout their history, and in later days wealthy Romans employed actors to walk in their family funeral processions wearing masks of their ancestors; or sometimes they carried wax masks or terracotta representations of their ancestors themselves. But early ceremonies concerned with the dead did not end with their cremation or burial. It was believed that their spirits lingered near the remains of the body in a state of half-life. These spirits were

*(National Museum, Budapest)
A Roman bronze mask of Juno
Lucina, the goddess of childbirth,
who retained her early Roman
nature. Her continuing
importance is indicated by the
fact that this comes from part
of the later Roman Empire, now
Hungary.*

45

called Manes, 'the good people', as a way of appeasing them; they could actually do great harm. They had to be sustained with food, and the remains of funeral meals have been found entombed with the dead. The food had to be renewed each year to prevent the Manes either wasting away or alternatively punishing the living for their neglect. On the anniversary of his mother's and father's deaths, therefore, every Roman had to honour them and ensure that they were supplied with food for the next year.

As well as the Manes, there were mischievous spirits of the dead of the whole household, called Lemures, who came back into the world on certain days in May. After midnight on those days, the father of the household walked through the house in his bare feet, throwing beans behind him so that he could feed the spirits without seeing them. He then beat a gong and the spirits vanished.

Early gods were not just concerned with the household. Each town or community probably had its own divinity who oversaw its activities. In Latium, villages seem to have grouped themselves together in cult-associations; for example Venus, originally a goddess of gardens, was worshipped at Lavinium, Diana at Lake Nemi and Jupiter Latiaris on the Alban Mount. Such divinities were not, however, at first conceived as living physically in the towns nor were they given temples in order to do so. They were, in a sense, guardian gods, perhaps a grander, urban version of the *genius loci*, or spirit of the place, who might be sensed presiding over a grove or a lake. Juno, who looked after the Etruscan town of Veii, was so successful that tradition has it that the Romans only succeeded in capturing Veii after they had ceremonially invoked her to leave that town for Rome. Many of these gods are now unknown, but may persist in place names. Cicero, who lived in the first century BC, claimed that he had seen religious diversity disappearing during his lifetime, but many local gods must have vanished earlier during the gradual Romanization of the Italian peninsula.

Not all gods were domestic or merely local, although some may have begun as local gods who, in the state-cult, grew into protectors of the whole community. The Italian tribes were Indo-European people, just as the Greeks were, and some of their gods may have originated many centuries earlier. The most important of these was Jupiter, or Iuppiter, the father of gods and men, the first part of whose name is linguistically similar to Zeus in Greek and Dyauspiter in Sanskrit, words connected with the light of day; the second part of the name is a version of *pater*, meaning father in Latin. He was thus a sky god in Rome, just as he was in Greece, but he existed in Italy quite separately from the Greek god.

In Rome, Jupiter was associated with two other gods – Mars and Quirinus. Mars, a god of war, was particularly important in this military state. He is also associated with agriculture, either because he was connected with fertility or, as some people think, because the activities of the soldiers he inspired allowed agriculture to continue. Mars came to have especial importance in Rome because he fathered Romulus and Remus, the city's founders. The Roman year began in March, his month, which was also the month in which military campaigns were resumed after the winter withdrawal. Quirinus was a very early god, who may have been Sabine in origin. He is also associated with war, but his name has similarities to the word adopted to describe the assembly of Roman citizens, 'Quirites'. His association with the city of Rome was strengthened when Romulus, after his death and apparent ascent to the heavens, was assimilated with him.

Some other great gods seem to have existed in Rome before the advent of Greek influence. Vesta has already been mentioned, and the goddess of the hearth is an early deity in many cultures for obvious reasons: from the hearth comes heat, food, comfort. The temple dedicated to her in Rome, which housed the city's own symbolic hearth, was built in a round shape and given a thatched roof, in imitation of the earliest hut dwellings in the city.

Janus, the god of the doorway, has already been mentioned. Like Vesta, he has no myth, but in his case it was because, although he remained important to the Romans, he had no Greek equivalent.

Vulcan, a fire-god, was probably introduced to Rome in quite early times, and Diana, a goddess of wild nature, was probably Italic. Minerva, who is thought by most people to have been an Italic goddess of handicrafts, but by others to have been an Etruscan war goddess, became part of the triad of Jupiter, Juno and Minerva who later became closely associated and very important both in Rome and her Empire.

The goddess Bona Dea, the 'Good Goddess', was a very ancient Roman divinity, probably a fertility power, who was worshipped only by women. Her real name may once have been Fauna, and later myths were invented for her to explain the fact that no man might be present at her worship, and no myrtle nor wine might be used at it.

The early Roman gods had names, functions and divine power, but they did not have myths, families or personalities. Sometimes people who addressed them were not clear exactly who they were nor of what sex, and inscriptions have been found asking the help of whatever god or goddess might be in a place. Towards the end of the monarchy, when Rome appears to have been ruled by Etruscans, things began to change: first because of the Greek influence on the Etruscans, second because the Etruscans seem likely to have built the first temples in Rome that housed statues of the gods, which ensured that the gods would become identifiable in a new, much more physical way.

(Museo Nazionale Romano, Rome) The importance of funeral ceremonies is suggested by the funerary carriages shown on this sarcophagus.

CHAPTER FIVE
STATE RELIGION IN REPUBLICAN ROME

The traditional date for the foundation of the Roman Republic was 509 BC and even although historians now question that date, it seems certain that rule by kings came to an end somewhere near the turn of the sixth and fifth centuries BC. The Roman historian, Livy, asserts that, before he was deposed, the last Etruscan king of Rome had begun to build a temple on the Capitoline Hill and that it was dedicated in the first year of the Republic. The finds of archaeologists support his assertion in two respects: the date of the temple is about right and it appears to have been Etruscan in style. It was dedicated to the Etruscan triad of gods, Tinia, Uni and Menvra, that is to say Jupiter, Juno and Minerva.

Its significance to the story of the gods of Rome is that it was constructed to provide a home for the three gods, which meant that a cult statue of each god could reside in its own section, or *cella*, with Jupiter, the most important, in the middle.

In early Rome a *numen*, or divine spirit, could be worshipped out of doors where it was felt to reside, or at a turf altar, or at a shrine near a spring. It could be worshipped in the form of a stone – as Jupiter actually continued to be in Rome in the temple of Jupiter Feretrius (Jupiter 'the Striker') probably because the stone was perceived as one of Jupiter's thunderbolts. No statue was needed because the god had no corporal form. The Etruscans, on the other hand, represented the gods in human form and placed them within a temple. When they did this in Rome, the Romans took a step towards anthropo-morphism, the representation of gods in human shape, which was at that time completely typical of Greek gods, but not of Roman ones.

The cult statue of Jupiter in the Capitoline temple was probably made by the great Etruscan sculptor, Vulca of Veii, from terracotta. Jupiter was already worshipped by Latin tribes in Italy and as Jupiter Optimus Maximus, Jupiter the Best and Greatest, he became the state god of the people of Rome. Once his statue was placed in the temple

people could see his image rather than simply perceiving his powerful spirit.

Temples for the Greeks were never places in which a congregation worshipped; they were dignified and beautiful homes for gods, within which could be found their cult statues. Now this fashion had been spread to Rome by the Etruscans.

Before considering the subject of Greek influence on Roman gods in more detail, something should be said briefly about the religious practices of the Roman Republic, which incorporated into its pantheon new gods who seemed to have something useful to offer, or assimilated old gods to new ones when it seemed convenient to do so. The point of religious practices was to maintain equilibrium between the people and the powerful forces that governed their lives; if it were possible to discover additional deities who needed to be addressed on man's behalf, then the state could only benefit from the knowledge.

Just as the father of the household was responsible for keeping his dependents in a dutiful and successful relationship with the gods, so officials of the state interceded with the gods on behalf of their people, entering into what seems to us now like an almost contractual relationship with them. Most people probably continued to honour their household gods, but all their other religious obligations were conducted on their behalf by functionaries of the state at ceremonies they probably did not normally attend.

The basis of Roman religious practice was ritual. Rites were carried out in order to maintain the established order of things, to keep things going well, with a proper balance between the human and divine. The gods were powerful and unknown; they controlled nature and could bring flood or famine unless they were properly conciliated. Ritual was a way of ensuring permanent prosperity through maintaining the *pax deorum*, the peace of the gods, and it had to be conducted precisely.

Under the Republic, there was a precise order of priests, the most important of whom were not professionals but men who performed that duty as one among their other political offices. An office of Rex Sacrorum, king of religious rites, was created to maintain the tradition of the earlier priest-kings, but this gradually became a largely ceremonial office. More important was the Pontifex Maximus, literally the greatest bridge-maker, in other words the chief priest, under whose direction were the Augurs and the Pontiffs, the chief administrators of the state cult.

There were also individual priests, called Flamines, who were attached to particular deities,

the most important of whom was the Flamen Dialis, or priest of Jupiter. Special groups of priests also existed to perform particular functions. Among them were the Vestal Virgins, six women chosen from leading patrician families at the age of twelve, who served for thirty years, after which they were allowed to marry. Although their position was sought after and honoured, they were severely punished for infringements of their duty such as allowing the sacred fire to go out, and if a Vestal was found guilty of not being chaste she was buried alive. They lived in a building near the Forum and tended the holy fire that burnt perpetually in the Temple of Vesta, the symbolic hearth of Rome; they were responsible for making a special mixture of salt and meal from which cakes were made for offerings. The meal was kept, together with objects used in various sacred festivals, in their store house.

The rituals by which the priests attempted to maintain the city's peace with the gods were chiefly centred on sacrifice, prayer, and the divination of the

ABOVE
(Museo Nazionale Romano, Rome) Head of a statue of the Emperor Augustus shown as Pontifex Maximus, or chief priest. He piously wears his toga over his head as though about to offer sacrifice.

OPPOSITE
(Villa Giulia, Rome) Life-size terracotta statue of Apollo from an Etruscan temple at Veii. This was probably made by the Etruscan sculptor, Vulca, who is said to have been called to Rome by Tarquinius Superbus to make the statue and decorations for the Temple of Jupiter on the Capitoline Hill. Late 6th-early 5th century BC.

will of the gods. Sacrifice meant literally the making of something *sacrum* or sacred, setting it aside to be the exclusive property of a god, which involved killing it if it was living. Sacrifice was designed to honour the god, and sometimes to expiate, or atone for, a wrong done by man. Lustrations, or processions to keep away hostile spirits, also sometimes culminated in sacrifice. Vows made to the gods before an action was undertaken were often completed by a sacrifice when the action had been successfully accomplished.

In the state cult, sacrifices had to be made scrupulously according to strictly observed rules. For example, the priest must have purified his hands and the offering must be acceptable; no contaminating intruder (such as a dog or a woman) must be present; there should be no intrusive noise, for which reason sacrifice was accompanied by music designed to block out any other noise. The priest making the sacrifice had to cover his head; this was an interesting difference from the more joyful Greek practice where the priest kept his head uncovered in order to open himself to the influence of the god. In meticulous Rome, if any mistake was made in the sacrifice, or if the god was wrongly addressed, the whole thing had to be repeated.

Many animals were sacrificed in Rome according to strictly laid-down rules. White beasts were used for gods of the upper world and black ones for those of the underworld. A set combination of animals formed the so-called *suovetaurilia* sacrifice that was often represented on stone carvings. They were a pig (*sus*), a sheep (*ovis*) and a bull (*taurus*). There were times of celebration or despair in the city when many sacrifices were called for; the altars of the Capitol must have run with blood and the air would have been heavy with the smell of butchery.

Prayer was also surrounded by rules. The right god had to be chosen and his or her attention had to be caught. That could only be achieved by addressing the deity by the correct name for the function he or she was requested to perform. Since many gods had a variety of names and might fail to respond if they were wrongly addressed, a number of names were sometimes listed at the beginning of a prayer; occasionally desperate formulae such as 'to the responsible deity' or 'whether you be god or goddess' are found on inscriptions. Prayers display great anxiety on the part of the Romans to keep the gods benevolently on their side.

Divination, or the skill of discovering the will of the gods from natural phenomena, was part of religion from early times in Rome. It became particularly important, however, as a result of Etruscan influ-

ence. The Etruscans held a number of books related to religious ritual that they believed had been revealed to them in early days. Among these rituals were those for interpreting such signs as thunder and lightning, which were thought to foretell events in man's everyday life.

The College of Augurs in Rome were responsible for divining whether or not circumstances were auspicious before undertaking certain events. The word *augur* may be connected with the Latin word for bird, and it was primarily from birds that the augurs derived their information, just as Romulus and Remus did when they sought to discover which of them should be leader in their new city. The sky was quartered according to the plan of the augurs, who watched to see which birds appeared in each quarter; they watched for certain kinds of birds; they even watched to see how chickens fed; all these things had significance. The writer, Cicero, who was appointed to the office of Augur, admitted in a letter that he thought augury was nonsense, yet the office was a prestigious one and he continued to perform it.

Augury gave way to some extent to haruspicy, at which the Etruscans excelled. The *haruspex* was a man who could discover divine intention by careful-

ly examining the entrails of beasts who had been sacrificed. The books of the *Etrusca disciplina*, or Etruscan discipline, include one that instructed professional *haruspices* in this art. A bronze model of a liver, divided up and inscribed with the names of Etruscan deities, has been found, which suggests that this craft, too, was governed by very specific rules.

As it can be seen, these habits were very close to superstition, and superstitious fear was marked too in the Roman attitude to omens, or prodigies of nature, such as large hailstones, particular kinds of lightning, deposits of sand by an unusual wind; anything out of the ordinary could portend disaster.

The state regulated the city's year through its calendar of festivals. This also set out which days were ordinary, *fas*, and which were *nefas*, days on which no business might be transacted. Many of these were days when festivals took place, some of them to do with honouring and placating the dead, or with ritual purification. It seems likely that these non-working days covered about a third of the year, but people would not have been expected to be present at most of the ceremonies, which would have been conducted on their behalf by the appropriate priests.

(*Yorkshire Archaeological Society Museum, York*) *This Roman altar found in York has the following comprehensive dedication: 'To the African, Italian and Gallic mother goddesses, Marcus Minucius Andens, soldier of the Sixth Legion Victrix... willingly, gladly and deservedly fulfilled this vow.'*

mary of great deeds of the past.

Some festivals also appear to have been genuinely popular, and in most cases these were ancient survivals from a rural tradition whose origin was no longer within the grasp of memory or understanding. Certain myths were created partly in an attempt to understand them.

The Lupercalia is an obvious example of a festival that dates back to a forgotten rite, yet it continued to be celebrated until it was stopped by a Christian bishop in the fifth century AD. Its name suggests an association with *lupus*, wolf, and it has been thought to have originated in an ancient cult intended to keep the forest wolves away from sheep folds in the clearings. In Republican Rome it was essentially a lustration, a purifying procession round the Palatine Hill, designed to ward off threatening spirits, but it took a strange traditional form, which suggests that it arose from some much earlier rite. On 15 February two teams of young men, chosen from patrician families, and called Luperci for this occasion, came together in a cave called the Lupercal on the Palatine Hill, a cave that some people associated with the twin founders of Rome, Romulus and Remus. Near the cave they sacrificed goats and a dog, in itself a very unusual sacrifice. The blood on the knife was smeared on the foreheads of two of the Luperci and wiped off again with a piece of wool soaked in milk. The men had to laugh at that point, although no one knew why. In the cave the Luperci then had a feast accompanied by a good deal to drink. They emerged into the February air dressed only in pieces of the goat's skin. In their hands they carried strips or thongs of the skin. Great crowds gathered at this point to watch the young men run a race along a marked course at the foot of the Palatine Hill. As they ran, they used their strips of goat skin like whips, flicking them at people. It was thought that these flicks promoted fertility so women who wanted to have children stood in their way as the Luperci passed.

March, the month of Mars, which marked the beginning of the campaign season for the army and of the agricultural year for farmers, was originally the first month of the Roman year. The priests celebrated a number of festivals to Mars, the god of war who was also a god of agriculture, during the early part of the month. The popular ceremonial was supplied by the dancing priests called Salii, who were twelve elected young patrician men. On 1 March they retrieved from the sanctuary of Mars in the *regia*, or old palace in the Forum, twelve bronze figure-of-eight shields, reminiscent of Mycenaean shields from Bronze Age Greece. One of these was

National pride was, however, encouraged in the citizen by the occasional public ceremonies of triumphal processions and the funerals of important men. Triumphal processions came to be granted to victorious generals, who had to have been responsible for at least 5000 deaths, and the processions became great public holidays. Officers of state accompanied the general and his army who paraded their spoils of war in processions that sometimes included singing and dancing. Funeral processions concluded with orations in praise of the dead man and all his ancestors, which provided a public sum-

said to have fallen from the sky on a distant 1 March and to have been copied on divine instructions by a blacksmith at the time. The young men, dressed in a sort of Bronze Age uniform, danced through the streets, following a traditional route, singing a song whose words no one could any longer understand. They stopped for a celebratory dinner at a different house each night. The shields were finally returned on 24 March, when the celebration came to an end.

Distant memories of human sacrifice were perhaps recalled at a festival in May. This was the completion of an earlier event in March, when puppets or dolls made of rushes or straw were put into 27 small shrines called *sacra Argeorum* that were distributed throughout the city. At the May festival the pontiffs, Vestal Virgins and the Priestess of Jupiter, dressed in mourning instead of her usual wedding dress, led a procession round the shrines to collect the puppets. They then took them solemnly to the wooden bridge near the Palatine and threw them into the river Tiber. A number of theories have been put forward to account for this ritual, which was apparently a popular one. Most suggest that it was a purification ceremony, some that old men had been sent to their death from the bridge in an earlier time, and others that the puppets were an offering to the river god to placate it for the indignity of having its river spanned by a bridge.

The Vestialia, or celebration of the cult of Vesta, was held in June, probably over the course of a week. The Vestal Virgins not only kept the sacred flame going throughout the year but also presided over a store-house, their version of the *penus*, or store-cupboard of every Roman family. This was usually kept locked, and opened only by the Vestals and the Pontifex Maximus. On 9 June each year, married women came to it in procession, bringing items of daily food as offerings. Later, the day came to be celebrated as a holiday for bakers, probably because of the special salted flour which the Vestals made for sacred rituals. June 15 was the day when the Vestals cleaned out their storehouse completely, taking any rubbish down to the river. This ceremony ended the ritual part of the day, and the Roman calendar states that the day should become a working day again as soon as the rubbish had been cleared away.

The final popular ceremony of the year, which had begun as a native agricultural feast of thanksgiving, was the Saturnalia, whose name shows that it had once been associated with the divinity Saturn, who in early Roman times was associated with sowing seed and preventing blight. From 217 BC it became more light-heartedly Greek in tone. It was celebrated on 17 December, after the autumn sowing had ended. Its original significance was clearly lost on urban Romans, but it had become and remained popular as an easy-going winter festival, which has provided the foundation for a number of western Christmas customs. The festival began with a sacrifice followed by a public banquet in the Forum. People stopped working, dressed informally and strolled about the streets. Gifts were exchanged and slaves were allowed considerable licence, even being waited on at table by their masters.

These are only a few of the more popular festivals celebrated in Rome during the course of the year. They show how tradition persisted when the early gods behind the original rites had been forgotten. They were festivals derived from the Di Indigetes, the native gods. Now it is time to account for the Hellenization of native gods and the acceptance of completely new gods.

BELOW
An Etruscan bronze plaque shows a haruspex *closely inspecting the entrails of an animal.*

The Appian Way was begun in 312
BC from Rome as far as Capua and
was later extended to Beneventum
and Brundisium, linking Rome with
the Greek colonies further south.
For the first part of the way it served
as a patrician cemetery and was
lined on either side by family graves
and statues.

CHAPTER SIX
THE INTRODUCTION OF NEW GODS INTO REPUBLICAN ROME

T hrough the centuries of the Roman Republic, the state gods were subject to strong Greek influence. The anthropomorphic Greek gods were very different from the disembodied divine spirits of the Romans but when Roman gods were assimilated to Greek ones, they acquired their cults, their personalities, their established networks of family relationships, their developed myths and even specific items of their appearance.

It is important to remember, however, that the Roman peasant in the fields probably continued to call upon his rural deities and the freedman in the city to make offerings to his household gods. Most people leave no record of their lives and most people were probably relatively untouched by the changes to be seen in Roman temples and in the literature read by educated people. In fact, it is clear from their writing that certain educated men regarded the changes as mere fashion that did not affect them at any deep level.

Greek influence came not just through the Etruscans but through the tribes of Italy who had trading contact with the cities of Magna Graecia on the coast of southern Italy and Sicily. Hellenization was at its height in Rome from the fourth to the third centuries BC. This was a period when Greek culture itself had been strongly influenced by Alexander the Great and the notion of victory, and new cults centred on gods of war found their way to Rome, even the cult of Victory herself, to whom a temple was dedicated. Rome probably absorbed most Greek influence when it absorbed Campania, the area of

LEFT
(British Museum, London) Roman bronze figure of Hercules.

OPPOSITE
(Roman Forum) A winged Victory is shown on this detail from the Arch of Septimius Severus, erected in AD 203 in honour of the tenth anniversary of his accession, and in memory of his and his sons' victories.

ABOVE
(Museo Civico, Bologna) The twins
Castor and Pollux are shown with
their horses on this Roman relief.

OPPOSITE
(British Museum, London) Bronze
statuette of Mercury, who was
assimilated to the Greek god
Hermes. He is shown wearing the
hat and cloak of a traveller and
carrying a purse to symbolize the
money to be made from trade. His
speed of travel is indicted by his
winged sandals. 1st century AD.

Italy closest to the Greek cities. The importance of the link between the two cultures was made explicit in 312 BC by the building of the Via Appia, the great road from Rome to Capua.

The Romans took new gods into their religious system as they felt the need for them. As the city grew from an agricultural centre to a trading, manufacturing and mercantile base new kinds of help were needed from divine sources, and new gods were found to supply those needs. Greek influence can be seen in the institution of new state cults. One of the first of the Greek gods to come to Rome, possibly from Tibur, a nearby Latin city, was Heracles, whom the Romans called Hercules. His cult was centred on an altar in the Forum Boarium, the Cattle Market. He had not originally been worshipped as a god in Greece, but admired as a hero whose father was Zeus himself. His deification was a later addition to his myth, as were his numerous travels in the west where Greek colonists had settled.

Hercules was said to have arrived at the Tiber after his Tenth Labour, which had involved taking a herd of cattle from the monster Geryon, who lived in

the far west, and driving them home to Greece. As he rested by the river Tiber the cattle were stolen from him by a local shepherd called Cacus, whom Hercules killed, characteristically freeing the country from one of its tiresomely anti-social characters.

Once established in Rome he was adopted as a god with particular influence over commerce, possibly because he had actually been introduced there by Phoenician traders who associated him with their god, Melqart, and because merchants identified with his wanderings and liked the tough way he dealt with anyone who threatened to upset his progress.

The cult of the twin brothers Castor and Pollux was traditionally introduced in Rome in 499 BC, when they are said to have appeared in the Forum to announce a Roman victory against the Latins and the Tarquins at Lake Regillus. They had fought on the Roman side in the battle. A temple was dedicated to them in 484 BC. While they were in the Forum they watered their horses in the lake of Juturna, a female water deity.

The twins, the Dioscuri or 'sons of Zeus', were in Greek myth Castor and Polydeuces, the brothers

60

of Helen of Troy and Clytemnestra. All four children were born from a double conception by their mother Leda, who was inseminated by a god and a mortal on the same day. Jupiter, who desired her, had disguised himself as a swan in order to rape her while she was walking near a river. That night she slept as usual with her husband, Tyndareus. The Romans thought of Juturna, rather than Helen, as the sister of the twins, which might have resulted from an Etruscan attempt to make a convenient triad of Juturna, Castor and Pollux.

Worship of the two gods was already established in Latium, as is shown by a bronze plaque to them in Lavinium, dating to the sixth or fifth century BC. Some people identified them with the great gods, the Penates of the state, that had originally been taken from Samothrace to Troy and were then taken to Italy by Aeneas. Whatever the reason for their arrival in Rome, they became very popular gods there.

In 495 BC, during an economic decline, the cult of Mercury was introduced. His Greek equivalent Hermes was, among other things, the god of merchants and dealers of all kinds and he was presumably felt likely to be a useful influence on commerce during a slump.

The Greek god, Apollo, was known throughout the ancient Mediterranean world for his oracles at Delphi, Delos and Cumae, but he was introduced into Rome primarily as a healing god about the middle of the fifth century BC. In 293 BC, during a period when pestilence raged in Rome, Apollo's son, another healing god called Asclepius, was imported from Greece and was worshipped in Rome as Aesculapius .

From the Etruscans the Romans borrowed the notion of the consenting gods, the Dei Consentes, twelve deities who advised Jupiter on important decisions. The Romans identified them with the twelve most important Greek gods, giving them Latin names, except for Apollo, who was already known by his Greek name. Once the Roman gods had been assimilated to their Greek counterparts, they were assimilated also into their myths, and so took on the relationships that existed between the Greek gods. This meant that the original natures and functions of the Roman gods were largely forgotten.

Jupiter, like Zeus, had always been a sky god, and he retained this characteristic. In Greece, migrating people had taken the worship of Zeus to regions whose people worshipped a mother goddess called Hera, and they had both assimilated her cult to the new cult of Zeus and preserved her status by making her his wife. Consequently, when the Roman god-

(Museo Nazionale Romano, Rome)
Relief of Minerva, Jupiter and Juno, the triad of deities to whom the first Capitoline Temple was dedicated at the beginning of the Republican period. In later years, when groups of buildings characteristic of the Roman Capitol were built in cities throughout the empire, especially in France and Africa, one temple was always dedicated to this group of deities.

dess Juno, who represented the fertile power of women, was assimilated to the Greek goddess Hera, she automatically became the wife of the Roman god Jupiter on analogy with Hera and Zeus.

The Roman god Mars became increasingly the god of war rather than of agriculture because of his assimilation to the Greek god Ares, who was only a god of war. Because Minerva had been an Etruscan craft-goddess, she was assimilated to Athena, who was also a goddess of crafts, but thereafter she shared Athena's wisdom and her talent for war as well. Because Athena had been born from the head of Zeus, so Minerva became the daughter of Jupiter.

The Roman goddess Diana actually had a good deal in common with her Greek counterpart, Artemis, since both were goddesses of untamed nature. She was the sister of Apollo, a relationship

accorded to Diana too after her assimilation. The Roman goddess Venus underwent a greater change. She had once been an ancient spirit of cultivated growth, whose name was neither masculine nor feminine; she acquired a much wider area of influence and more glamorous persona through her assimilation to the goddess Aphrodite, the most beautiful of the Greek goddesses, who was the wife of Hephaestus and the lover of Ares. Venus thus became the wife of Vulcan, the *numen* of volcanoes, who was assimilated to the god Hephaestus, the smith, whose fiery work had been suggested by his own early association with volcanoes. She also acquired Mars as a lover on analogy with Aphrodite's adultery with Ares.

The twelve important gods and their counterparts are set out here:

Gods		Goddesses	
Greek	**Roman**	**Greek**	**Roman**
Zeus	Jupiter	Hera	Juno
Poseidon	Neptune	Athena	Minerva
Ares	Mars	Artemis	Diana
Apollo	Apollo	Aphrodite	Venus
Hephaestus	Vulcan	Hestia	Vesta
Hermes	Mercury	Demeter	Ceres

(Bardo Museum, Tunis) Roman mosaic of Diana, the huntress, that illustrates the characteristics she shared with the Greek goddess Artemis. 2nd century AD.

In spite of these assimilations, the Romans continued their habit of worshipping spirits by making shrines and temples to such abstractions as Salus – Health, Fides – Faith, Pietas – dutifulness to the gods, and Moneta – the spirit of the Mint, from which came prosperity. The persistence of this habit suggests a surviving desire to worship in a Roman rather than a Greek way.

Following the early assimilations of the Roman to the Greek gods, over a period of about two hundred years during the Republic new gods and rituals were deliberately introduced to Rome by the Senate, almost as part of policy, at times of crisis when there was need to reassure and quieten the people by diverting them. It seems possible that Livy might have had his own experience of this policy in mind when he made Numa, traditionally the second king of Rome, say of his unruly people that he would find a way to 'inspire them with the fear of the gods.'

It was perhaps in this spirit that the *duoviri sacris faciundis*, the two men who were nominated from the ruling class to be in charge of arranging the sacred rites and who became the *decemviri*, or ten men, in 367 BC, were sent at times of unusual portents or great danger to consult the Sibylline Books. These were said to be the works of the Sibyl, a prophetess of Apollo who presided over his oracle at Cumae.

In early histories of Rome the story goes that she offered nine oracular books to Tarquinius Priscus, king of Rome, but he twice foolishly refused them; on each occasion she destroyed three books and raised the price of the remaining ones and he was finally constrained to buy the remaining three at three times the price of the original nine. It was these books that the *decemviri sacris faciundis* consulted at times of crisis in Rome.

The priests may, in early times, actually have visited the oracle at Cumae, but by about 367 BC the books seem to have been preserved in the Temple of Jupiter on the Capitoline. They were burnt in a fire that destroyed the Temple in 82 BC, then reassembled from a number of sources. The new books, containing oracles written in Greek verse, were copied and kept in two gold chests in the temple of Apollo on the Palatine. Only the *decemviri* were allowed to consult the books, and their advice was almost always followed. The cynical commentator is bound to wonder what convenient adjustments might have been made to the books at various times, but there seems no doubt that their instructions to the Senate to innovate popular rituals at a number of difficult times helped to pacify the populace; and a chief requirement of Roman religion was that it should

establish a peaceful relationship between men and the gods.

When there was famine in the city in 496 BC, the Books advised that a cult of Ceres, Liber and Libera should be introduced. These were early Roman gods, who had previously been conceived as individual spirits of fertility, but they were now brought together as cult figures in a way that parallelled the cult of the Greek corn and wine deities – Demeter, the goddess of grain and the harvest, Dionysus, the god of wine, and Kore, or Persephone, the daughter of Demeter. In introducing this cult, the Senate was departing from its normal intention to keep Roman religion as free as possible from alien influences. Through the cult Romans gradually became acquainted with the Greek story of Persephone's seizure by Hades, who ruled over the Underworld, the barren period on earth during Demeter's search to find her, and the renewal of the process of growth when Persephone returned. These were the elements of the Eleusinian Mysteries, a Greek cult concerning the after-life that took hold in Rome in later years, in spite of disapproval from the authorities.

The Roman historian, Varro, says that the temple to Ceres, Liber and Libera dedicated in 493 BC, was the first to have a Greek rather than an Etruscan statue. Its immediate importance to the ordinary people was that it became the centre of the Roman corn trade.

In 433 BC, during a time of pestilence, a temple was dedicated to Apollo, a healing god. In 399 BC there was pestilence again in Rome when a hot summer followed a particularly severe winter. This time the Sibylline Books suggested an innovation called a *lectisternium*, from the word *lectus*, meaning the couch on which people reclined at meals. The idea was that a feast should be offered to the gods in public. It was a development of an annual Greek celebration when the gods were invited to dine in person with humans but it took a more spectacular form in Rome. During a period of eight days, images of six Greek gods, known by their Latin names of Apollo and Latona (the mother of Apollo and Diana), Hercules and Diana, Mercury and Neptune, were presented to the public. They were displayed reclining on couches, with food and drink spread on tables before them. Everyone in the city was free to see the images and to use the eight days as a holiday in which they might offer hospitality at their own doors, even to strangers.

Five such ceremonies were decreed in the fourth century and presumably offered both a diversion and an opportunity for closer acquaintance with the gods,

who must have seemed very different, displayed on their couches, from the formerly invisible Roman *numina*, or divine spirits.

The years of the second Punic War (218-201 BC), when Hannibal led the forces of Carthage against Rome, were very difficult ones. Rome was defeated on a number of occasions and the populace feared that Hannibal would attack Rome itself. After the defeat of the Romans at Lake Trasimene in 217 BC, the Senate consulted the Sibylline Books, which ordained the introduction of certain rites to calm the people.

Great Games to Jupiter were to be instituted, and a temple built to the Venus of Eryx; another *lectisternium* should be held, together with a *supplicatio*, and there should be a *ver sacrum*. This was all done. *Supplicatii*, which tended to be held alongside *lectisternia*, were occasions when the population, wearing garlands, went in procession round the shrines of the city, prostrating themselves in a manner that would normally have been considered hysterical and un-Roman, although perhaps typically Greek. The *ver sacrum*, the custom of the Sacred Spring, had been a very early custom in Italy. When a community grew to the extent that there was insufficient land to support it, a whole year's cohort of young adults were dedicated to a god and sent off to find land for a new home somewhere else. In this new Roman version of the custom, all the animals born that spring were sacrificed to the gods.

All this was followed in 216 BC by a new instruction from the Sibylline Books after the Romans' worst defeat at the Battle of Cannae. In order to expiate whatever wrongs the gods were punishing Rome for, it was decreed that a Greek man and woman and a Gaulish man and woman should be buried alive in the Forum Boarium, the cattle market. The historian Livy found this action disgusting and

'hardly Roman'. In fact, it had something in common with an aspect of Etruscan religion that was normally eschewed by the Romans and the Greeks. Etruscan wall-paintings show that in their later period they were much preoccupied with the torments of the dead at the hands of the demons of the underworld. It seems that they offered human sacrifices to appease the demons, commonly setting their victims to fight each other in duels. This custom appears to have become a model for the much later gladiatorial contests in Rome.

Under pressure of war, the Senate had sanctioned another alien rite in 249 BC, which it repeated in 207 BC when it arranged a festival to appease the Greek deities of the Underworld, Hades and Persephone, under their Roman names of Dis and Proserpina; in this also they seem to have been following Etruscan rather than Roman tradition.

The pontiffs continued to record numerous disturbing prodigies and omens of disaster in those years, and it was clearly felt that the gods had not yet been appeased. A new *lectisternium* was held, on a larger scale, at which twelve pairs of gods, both Greek and Roman were displayed. In an important break with tradition, for the first time no distinction was made between the native gods and foreign ones.

This open attitude to the introduction of foreign gods persisted as long as it suited the Senate to distract the people. Interest in oriental gods, which was surfacing among the mixed population of Rome, could be said to have been officially recognized in Rome during this period of crisis. In 205 BC, the Senate unearthed a prophecy that a foreign invader would be driven from Rome if the Great Mother were brought to the city.

The Great Mother was the Asiatic goddess, known in Rome as Cybele. An embassy was sent to Pessinus in Galatia, where she was worshipped, and King Attalus of Pergamum, unwilling to offend Rome, agreed to send her there. She arrived at Ostia in the following year, in the form of a black meteorite with which she was identified. She was greeted by Scipio and escorted to the Temple of Victory on the Palatine Hill by some of the most important aristocratic wives in Rome. The day, 4 April, was thereafter treated as a holiday and new Games, the Megalensia, were inaugurated.

The cult of Cybele was the last important official innovation based on the Sibylline Books, and it might be said to have been successful in that Rome defeated Hannibal. The Roman Senate had, however, introduced a foreign cult without fully understanding it.

Along with Cybele came her myth, which

OPPOSITE
(Naples Museum) This painting from a household shrine in Pompeii shows the god Dionysus, decked with grapes, standing before Mount Vesuvius whose lower slopes are covered with trellised vines. Vesuvius was famous for its wine, upon which the prosperity of Pompeii partly depended. The snake suggests that Dionysus is presented here as the genius loci *or spirit of the place.*

LEFT
A terracotta plaque showing a war elephant reminiscent of those used by Hannibal during the Second Punic War.

69

Fresco showing a group of children sacrificing to Diana. It might suggest that the Greek association of young, unmarried girls with the untamed, virginal Artemis, was transferred to Roman girls and Diana.

is a strange one with very mixed origins that show how Greek myths were interwoven with eastern ones as well. Zeus attempted to rape Cybele while she was sleeping. Although his seed fell to the earth, as an earth mother she received it and bore a child – a bisexual monster called Agdistis. Dionysus, the god of wine, made Agdistis drunk and tied his sexual organs to a tree so that when he awoke from his drunken stupor and tried to get up he castrated himself.

A tree grew from his blood and one day the daughter of a river god picked some fruit from the tree, which she put in her lap to hold. The fruit impregnated her. When she gave birth, her father first tried to kill her and then to expose the baby. Cybele intervened to prevent this. When the child, called Attis, had grown into a handsome young man Cybele fell in love with him and he is often shown as her companion. He was unfaithful to her, however, and she sent him mad. During a fit of madness he castrated himself under a pine-tree, where he bled to death. Like other vegetation gods, he rose again and his rite included ceremonies both of mourning and of the joyful renewal of life.

What the Roman Senate had not realized was that the priests of Cybele were eunuchs and that their initiation to her service included self-castration while they were in an ecstatic trance. In later years the Senate forbade Roman citizens to take part in the orgiastic rites of the goddess.

The aristocracy had brought the situation on themselves; they had exploited their position by encouraging the introduction of new gods, festivals and games when it suited them to distract the people's attention from the disastrous events of the Punic War. After the war, however, the Senate reversed its policy and, in general, tried to prevent foreign influences from invading the state religion. They continued to maintain the *pax deorum* on behalf of the people, but the state religion had by now become ossified and its ceremonies rigid. The Senate kept a careful eye on more exotic forms of worship, such as that of Cybele, and decreed that they should be conducted privately. Their main fear was, as usual, of disorder among the teeming populace.

Therefore in 186 BC measures were taken throughout Italy against the cult of Bacchus that was becoming increasingly popular: no one was to be an officer of the cult and no more than five people were to take part in its ceremonies. Bacchus, who had long been known in Rome as Liber, was the name used for the Greek god Dionysus in his particular aspect as a god associated with wine and uninhibited behaviour. Because he was a vegetation god, his cult was also connected with fertility, death and rebirth. His cult could only be entered through initiation, during which certain mysteries were revealed to the initiates. Celebration of the cult involved drinking and orgiastic dancing. It had spread very quickly from southern Italy and fears that its orgiastic nature might disturb public order and its initiation mysteries encourage the growth of groups of dissidents with secret views made the Senate treat its member-

Cybele and Attis. Cybele, the Great Mother, is often shown in a chariot drawn by lions. Attis wears a Phrygian cap, which denotes his oriental origin, and leans against the pine tree that forms a crucial part of his legend. Roman altar from Asia Minor, end of the 3rd century AD.

ship as a political offence rather than a religious one.

Although the Republican Senate banned the cult it became popular again under the Empire, and the process of initiation is openly illustrated in some wall paintings of the first century AD at Pompeii.

The state religion had probably never been intellectually satisfying to educated men, although they subscribed to the sense of duty to the well-being of the state that it promoted. They seem to have found some comfort in Greek philosophy, which had found its way to Rome by this period. Two schools of philosophy appear to have been most influential, the Epicurean and the Stoic, of which the Stoic school proved the more lasting.

The philosophy of Epicurus, a fourth-century Greek, did not change very much over time. It was based on a current scientific theory that all matter consisted of streams of atoms flowing in parallel channels that occasionally swerved and so produced new combinations. There might be gods, but they had nothing to do with life, which ceased completely with death when the atoms of the soul dissolved. The chief aim of life was pleasure, not necessarily hedonistic pleasure, but freedom from pain, ambition and power, and the cultivation of the joys of friendship and a quiet life. The arrival of his philosophy in Rome unfortunately coincided with a period of material wealth, which meant that Epicurean notions of pleasure were too often interpreted as self-indulgence.

A number of Epicurean philosophers were

expelled from Rome in 173 BC, which suggests that the authorities were disturbed by their views. Nevertheless Epicurus influenced the poets Lucretius and Horace, and Virgil also shows awareness of his ideas.

Stoicism developed from the ideas of Zeno, a Phoenician, who was so poor that he taught in the Porch, or Stoa, of the market in Athens. His ideas were later disseminated in Rome by Panaetius, who developed them in a way that made a specific appeal to Romans. Stoicism saw the universe as governed by law, which the good man must obey. Stoics were pantheists, who saw god in everything, although he might be called by many names, such as Zeus, Jupiter, Nature, Fire, Breath or Logos (the Word). It was a determinist philosophy, seeing man's actions, but not his will, as fixed. It was also a philosophy of acceptance. It saw man as having within himself some of the divine spark; this governed his behaviour, and made him rule his own life with reason. The fact that it could therefore be applied to man's daily actions and decisions seems to have appealed to the practical Romans. It survived to be an influence even on some Christians.

By the end of the Republic, the introduction of foreign gods had led to the recognition of gods in human shape and to the unquestioned assimilation of Roman gods to Greek ones. It had also led to a far more emotional and intense method of worship than Roman rituals had so far supplied. Cybele was the first deity to be introduced from the East, but it was from that direction that new gods would come in future, including of course the God of the Christians. Educated men seem to have turned away from the new emotionalism and towards philosophy, and this, in turn, tended towards the notion of one god and therefore also prepared the way for Christianity.

(Vatican Museums, Rome) This statue of Augustus shows him in his role as leader of the Roman army. The decoration of his breastplate is used to evoke various mythological and historical references. The figure of the Sky spreads his cloak across the top of the breastplate. Beneath him Sol, the Sun, drives his chariot towards Aurora, the Dawn, who rides off on a winged female figure. At the bottom rests the goddess Tellus, Earth. Above her, to the left and right, Apollo rides a griffin and his sister Diana a stag. The two figures in the centre probably represent Augustus's success in persuading the Parthians to return Roman legionary standards they had captured thirty years earlier. The cupid supporting the Emperor's right leg is the son of Venus and may suggest Augustus's own descent from her through the Julian family. The dolphin may refer to the emperor's victory at the sea battle of Actium. The statue is from Livia's villa at Prima Porta, Rome.

CHAPTER SEVEN
THE GODS OF THE ROMAN EMPIRE

When Octavius Caesar, the adopted son of Julius Caesar, returned to Rome in 29 BC he was acclaimed as a Prince of Peace who had not only won a foreign war but also brought to an end a long period of civil strife. A triple triumph celebrated his conquest of Illyricum, his victory at Actium and the consequent annexation of Egypt to Rome. In 27 BC, his choice of the title Augustus under which to rule was a felicitous one, carrying with it suggestions of a revered man who was consecrated to his task. In 23 BC he was recognized as Emperor. In 12 BC, on the death of the current Pontifex Maximus, or Chief Priest, he was elected to that office, and in 2 BC he was given the title Pater Patriae, Father of the Fatherland.

In the spirit of that title, he stressed the importance of the family, and sought to reform the institutions of the state. For some time the state had neglected its regular religious observances and many temples had fallen into disrepair. Some satirists were making mocking references to the gods in their plays; other writers of the period, however, expressed their belief that Rome could not be great unless piety was restored to the state. Augustus shared this view, and set himself to renew the state cults, first by overseeing the necessary repair and rebuilding of eighty-two neglected temples.

Rather than looking to the new gods and religions that were spreading into Italy from the East, Augustus looked back to the more traditional gods of Rome in his attempts to inspire dutiful worship, or *pietas*, in his people. He had long shown a particular

enthusiasm for the worship of Apollo, who appeared to him and supported him at the battle of Actium, and he had founded a temple to him on the Palatine Hill in 36 BC. Now he propagated his worship, not just in his aspect as a god of healing, but as the inspiration for a progressive, peaceful civilization that would cast a new light on the world. In the Hellenistic world, Apollo had by this time become associated with the sun, an appropriate image for the dawning of a new age in Rome. There is a famous statue of Augustus made to stand at the Prima Porta; he is wearing armour, and on his breastplate are figures of the sun and the goddess of dawn.

Augustus also stressed the cult of Mars, particularly in two aspects: first as the father of Romulus, the founder of Rome, and second as Mars Ultor, the Avenger. As a young man, in 42 BC, he had vowed a temple to Mars in a spirit of vengeance for the murder of Julius Caesar. In 2 BC he dedicated a temple to Mars Ultor, expressing the hope that every young man would worship there at the beginning of his military career, and every commander before setting out on an expedition.

The prophetic words of the ghost of Anchises, the father of Aeneas, in the *Aeneid* have already been quoted in an earlier chapter, saying that the arts of the Romans should be to pacify, to impose the rule of law and to spare the conquered while at the same time beating down the proud. Through the two gods, Apollo and Mars, Augustus promoted the twin notion of the spread of Roman civilization and its support by just war. The joint themes were spread

Remains of the temple in Rome dedicated to Mars Ultor (the Avenger) by Augustus in 2 BC. It was a centre for great ceremonies and served as the Imperial Sanctuary.

among educated people by writers of his period, particularly by Virgil.

The Ara Pacis, or Altar of Peace, dedicated in 13 BC, which can still be seen in Rome today in a restored form, presents a similar vision of Rome through its scenes of family worship, religious processions and the arrival of Aeneas in Italy.

Augustus took these ideas to a wider public by means of the Secular Games in 17 BC. These Games were, by tradition, thought to be held every hundred years, but had not in fact been held since 263 BC. The holding of the Games was intended to suggest that a new *saeculum*, or age, was about to begin, and that idea was reinforced by the occurrence of a number of contemporary prophecies about the beginning of a new Golden Age. The games, together with bloodless sacrifices to the Fates, the goddess of childbirth, Mother Earth, Jupiter Optimus Maximus, Juno and Apollo, and hymns to the gods sung by choirs of young people, lasted for three days. As intended, they presumably carried Augustus's message of renewed piety, peace and greater prosperity to most of the population of Rome.

It is scarcely surprising that, after his death, Augustus, like his adoptive father, Julius Caesar, was declared a god himself. It had long been a feature of Greek and Roman religion that exceptional men, at the end of their lives, might be taken into the pantheon of gods; it had happened to the Greek Heracles and the Roman Romulus. Both of them, however, had one divine parent. Alexander the Great had asked for, and been given, recognition of his divinity, mainly as an astute way of establishing his power in his Eastern and Egyptian empires, where kingship and divinity went hand in hand. In Egypt the king had for many centuries also been a god. After Alexander's death the Greek dynasty he founded in Egypt, the Ptolemies, established a cult of the reigning monarch to ensure their position there.

Augustus ruled Egypt as part of the Roman Empire, so he was perforce a divine emperor there. His adoptive father, Julius Caesar, had believed he had a personal association with the goddess Venus because, as a member of the Julian family, he was directly descended from Iulus, or Ascanius, the son of Aeneas, who was himself the son of Venus and Anchises. Augustus never claimed divinity directly, but he allowed himself to be called *divi filius*, son of the god, that is of the divine Julius. His birthday became a public holiday and a month was named after him. He also encouraged the development of two cults that led towards the recognition of his divinity: one was the Numen Augusti, the Divine Will of Augustus, to which altars have been found

A statue of the god Apollo stands in front of the temple dedicated to him in Pompeii. Apollo was one of the most popular gods in Imperial Rome. Vesuvius can be seen in the background.

dedicated as far away as Gaul and Africa; the other was a cult to his Genius, which was invoked at the taking of oaths.

After Augustus died, in September, AD 14, the Senate agreed that the Divine Augustus should be accepted among the gods of the state. A senator claimed to have seen him bodily ascending to the sky. At his funeral, Tiberius compared Augustus with Hercules as a great benefactor to the whole world.

The deification of the Emperor after his death set a pattern for the future, although certain Emperors – for example, Tiberius, Caligula, Nero and Domitian – did not achieve the status, while others pressed for divine recognition during their life-time. The story is often quoted of the Emperor Vespasian joking on his death-bed, 'Oh dear, I think I'm becoming a god.' The Emperor Hadrian actually had his young favourite, Antinous, deified after his death by drowning. The emperor-cult became particularly important in the furthest reaches of the Empire where local people often joined it with the cult of the goddess Roma in an attempt to emphasize their attentiveness to the power of Rome. Its practice in such places was presumably encouraged as one element in the Romanization of the diverse cultures of the Empire.

Julius and Augustus Caesar both associated themselves strongly with a god, Julius with Venus and Augustus with Apollo and, through him, with images of the sun. A study of Roman sculpture and coins will show that later Roman Emperors went further than this and actually identified themselves with particular gods; Caligula went through most of the pantheon, and ordered that his head should replace that of Zeus at Olympia. Nero was identified with Zeus the Giver of Freedom and Hadrian with Zeus Olympius. This habit sometimes extended to their families; for example Julia Domna, the wife of Septimius Severus, who came from a royal priestly family in Syria, was identified with Cybele, and depicted on the throne of Juno.

It has already become clear that Roman religion was not exclusive and that it was possible, even desirable, to worship more than one god. As Rome extended its empire, a greater variety of gods became available for worship and more assimilations of one god to another were made. In this confusing situation, certain new forms of worship spread through parts of the empire and to Rome itself.

One group of gods came from Egypt. They were the family of Osiris and Isis, their son Horus and their servant, the jackal-headed Anubis. Ptolemy 1, the Greek ruler of Egypt, knowing the resistance of both Greeks and Romans to the notion of animal gods, added to the group what amounted to an artificially created god – Serapis (or Sarapis in Greek). Serapis was originally to be found at Memphis, at the sanctuary where the dead bulls of Apis were entombed. Ptolemy merged the spirit of Apis, the sacred bull, with Osiris, the god of the dead, to produce a third deity Osorapis, or Serapis, around whom he created a cult that would enhance his own power. It was so successful in the Roman world that Serapis seems to have replaced Osiris there as the husband of Isis.

Early Egyptian stories make it clear that Isis and Osiris were originally fertility deities; Osiris represented the rising of the Nile flood-waters and Isis the land that awaited them. This particular fertility myth was, of course, fairly meaningless in countries whose fertility depended on rain rather than on the

Detail of a panel from the south side of the Ara Pacis Augustae *the Altar of the Augustan Peace, dedicated in 9 BC. It probably shows some of the people present at the inauguration ceremony, and it also illustrates the Roman ideal of pious and dignified family life. On the left of the procession,* flamines, *or priests, are recognizable from their distinctive caps, and an assistant at the sacrifice carries an axe. The central figure is probably Marcus Agrippa, a general, and later son-in-law to Augustus. To the right is the figure of the Empress Livia, and to the right of that is probably Tiberius, her son, the future emperor. The children are also thought to be members of the imperial family.*

Detail of the south-east panel of the Ara Pacis. The seated goddess is Tellus, Earth, perhaps perceived here as Italia, the personification of Italy. The children and the fruit on her lap suggest abundance. Breezes surround her and at her feet are healthy beasts, lush vegetation and an overturned urn that suggests the proximity of a spring. The elements of earth, air and water thus flourish in the Augustan peace.

power of a single river. The Roman cult of Isis, which was very different from its Egyptian original, became popular with groups of poorer freedmen and women in the city towards the end of the Republic, but the shrines of Isis and Serapis were destroyed on the orders of the Senate in 50 BC and they were kept outside the city limits of Rome after that until the Emperor Caligula admitted them into the official calendar during his reign (37-41 AD).

The Egyptian gods are thought to have been brought to Rome by sailors and merchants, and the mysteries of Isis became particularly popular among women. She was rapidly identified with the goddess Demeter/Ceres, the goddess of corn, and her mysteries had some similarities to the Eleusinian Mysteries of Greece that gave enlightenment about the afterlife and promised victory over the powers of night.

Other goddesses were assimilated with Isis. She can often be distinguished in statues, however, by her headdress; it sometimes shows the sun's disc sur-

rounded by a crescent moon, or a cow's horns, or the palm leaves of victory, or two feathers that represent the soul. She usually holds a *sistrum*, the rattle that was used in her ceremonies. She is sometimes identified with Tyche, that is the Roman goddess Fortuna, who usually holds a rudder to direct affairs and an overflowing cornucopia, or horn of plenty. The cult of Isis had a professional priesthood, and its processions and complex rites seem to have been popular.

The cult of Serapis persisted until the end of the fourth century AD, and appears to have become respectable in Rome. The Emperor Hadrian had a Serapeum constructed at his villa at Tivoli, outside Rome. Serapis was associated with the sun and the sky gods and yet, like Osiris, was also thought of as a god of the dead. He was even a healing god. On some inscriptions, his worshippers have gone the whole way and described him as 'One Zeus Serapis'.

From about the middle of the second century

AD, the Isis cult gave way to some extent, at least among men, to a new cult whose origins were in Persia, but which developed into what was essentially a Roman mystery cult. This was the cult of Mithras. It was strongly associated with astrology, as might be expected in a cult deriving from Persia, where Babylonian astrologers had been very influential. It clearly had links with Persian Zoroastrianism, which stressed dualism in life, the conflict between the forces of light and darkness.

The newly developed cult of Mithras carried a number of myths with it. One is frequently illustrated in the numerous statues of Mithras slaying a bull. It claimed that in the struggle between light and darkness, the Sun was the chief representative of the divinity Ahura-Mazda. Mithras supported Ahura-Mazda in his struggle against darkness and in the end took the supremacy from him, but with his agreement.

The first living thing created by Ahura-Mazda was a wild bull, which Mithras wrestled into submission, holding it by the horns. He then took it to an underground cave from which it escaped. The Sun sent his messenger, the Raven, to watch where it went and Mithras, guided by Ahura-Mazda, found it.

Mithras pulled back the bull's head and, clinging to its nostrils with his left hand, he sank a dagger into its throat with his right hand. From the flow of the bull's blood sprang all plant and animal life. Ahriman, the force of darkness, sent his servants – a scorpion, an ant and a snake – to drink up the life-creating blood, but it spread throughout the earth. The Sun therefore made a covenant with Mithras, before whom he bowed and by whom he was crowned. They parted after sharing a ceremonial feast, which was afterwards commemorated by adherents to the cult in a ritual sacramental meal.

The importance of the sun in Mithraism may well have encouraged the cult's popularity at that period. Mithras, who usually wears a Phrygian cap, is sometimes shown wearing a radiate crown, that is with a circlet on his head from which the sun's rays project. Such a crown was also shown on Serapis and on Alexander the Great. Some Roman emperors liked to present themselves wearing it on their coins. The dualism inherent in the cult might have made both an intellectual and an emotional appeal to Romans whose state religion had never presented good and evil as rival forces.

The cult also offered a complex ceremonial,

(National Museum, Ravenna) Relief showing the deification, or apotheosis, of Augustus, which was accorded to him after his death. He is accompanied by members of the Julio-Claudian family.

trained priests, an ethical code, a strong sense of fraternity among its participants, and secrecy. It advocated that its initiates should actively behave well rather than that they should merely abstain from wrong-doing. It was a religion exclusively for men, and it appealed above all to men from the upper classes of society, to business men, and particularly to military men, especially officers. It seems likely that a number of emperors actually encouraged its spread through Roman military camps, and evidence of its celebration has been found as far apart as England – on Hadrian's Wall and in London – and Africa. Some civilians took to Mithraism as well, but it seems to have been rather exclusive in its appeal.

Its exclusive nature must have been reinforced by its rites. These were celebrated in fairly small vaulted caves, where the ritual feasts were presumably held, but which cannot have held many people. Each cave was decorated with astrological signs, and represented an image of the universe. At one end there was usually a statue representing Mithras slaying the bull, an action which in itself seemed to be taking place in a cave and being watched by a raven.

There were secret initiation rites by which men rose through various grades, from the Raven – an observer, the Nymphus, or bride, and the Soldier up to the Lion, which appears to have been the standard grade. After that there were three further grades, the Persian, the Sun-runner and the Father. Each of these grades was protected by different planets or gods. The lions represented the fire that would burn the body after death, and through which the released soul would ascend to heaven.

One rite – the *taurobolium* – which has often been associated with Mithraism, is actually a rite of the Cybele cult, but may have been used in Mithraism at times. To celebrate this rite, a man went into a pit, above which a bull was sacrificed on a grid of some kind so that the man below was drenched in the blood of the animal. It seems possible that it has become associated with Mithraism after the event because of the bull sacrifice.

Some writers have seen Mithraism, with its dualism, one main god and ethical code as an important rival to Christianity. It seems rather to have been one of a number of religions to which some men turned at a time of intellectual and emotional religious enquiry when a ferment of ideas and cults were moving through Rome's vast Empire.

The Roman Empire gave its people religious freedom, and most people probably continued to worship their local divinities, just as most ordinary Romans probably continued to pay attention to their household gods rather than anything more exotic –

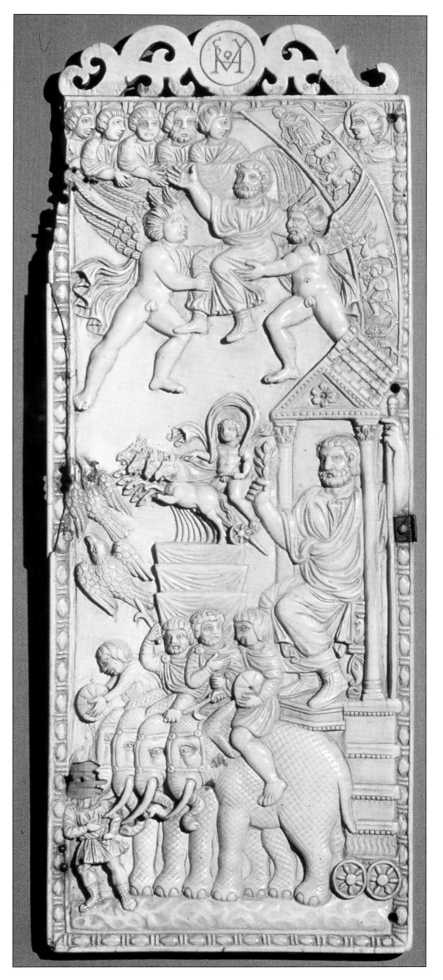

the household altars found below the volcanic ash in first century Pompeii certainly seem to suggest this. Because the religions of the empire were, for the most part, polytheisms that maintained their cults through the common practices of local festivals and sacrifice at local shrines, there was a good deal of possibility for the interchange and assimilation of gods.

As some of the more remote western provinces of the empire became more urbanized, they sometimes chose to give their gods a Roman gloss by introducing some sort of uniformity to them and using Roman names. This was known as the *interpretatio Romana*, where local gods were identified with Roman ones, but it could also work in reverse when Roman settlers abroad chose to use a local name for one of their own gods.

Julius Caesar noted that Mercury was very popular with the Gauls. The Roman god's name was applied to some of their gods where there was a very approximate resemblance between them. He was, for example, associated with the god Lug who gave his name to Lugdunum, modern Lyons. At Trier, there is an example of Mars Lenus, where Lenus, a local healing god has been assimilated to the Roman god. Mars was unsurprisingly one of the Roman gods most often invoked in Britain, since many of the Romans living there would at least at some stage in their lives have been soldiers. There are more than thirty inscriptions, for example, to Mars Coccidius at Bewcastle. Maponus, a British god of youth, was assimilated to Apollo. The Roman town of Bath was known as Aquae Sulis, which shows that the presiding goddess was felt to be the Celtic deity Sul, who was worshipped as a sun-goddess in that area.

Sometimes joint cults were set up, as when some Seine boatmen in Gaul in the reign of Tiberius made a four-sided monument to Esus, Tarvos, Vulcan and Jupiter, honouring two of their own gods together with two Roman ones. Some Celtic gods seem, however, to have kept their own identity, among them Cernunnos, the antler-headed god, and Epona, a goddess associated with the horse.

Roman influence was far less obvious in Greece, which tended to retain its own gods and mythology, already long-established before Rome existed. In Asia Minor, more foreign gods were Greek than Roman because of the influence of Alexander the Great as well as the ancient trading, social and cultural ties between Greece and Asia Minor.

Syria sent some of its gods to Rome; it had an enormous diversity of religions, largely because its mountain ranges created a series of unconnected terrains. The Syrian goddess Atagartis was brought to

Rome fairly early, probably by slaves. Under these circumstances, Syrian deities tended to become naturalized Roman ones, rather as Egyptian ones did. The god Melqart of Tyre, for example, became assimilated with Hercules, and Eshmun of Sidon with Asclepius, the Roman healing god, who was himself assimilated to the Greek Aesculapius. Eshmun was so well assimilated that he cured the sick by incubation, that is by sending them a dream of recovery as they slept, in precisely the same way as Aesculapius cured Greeks who slept near his shrine at Epidauros.

Another Syrian god, Jupiter of Doliche, named after a small town in Commagene near the upper Euphrates, was usually shown as a god of lightning, standing on a bull, holding a thunderbolt in one hand and a hatchet in the other. He was the patron of iron-workers and therefore popular with soldiers who must have frequently needed his help. Inscriptions have been found to him as far apart as Africa, Germany, Hungary and Britain.

In one of the stranger episodes of Roman history, a fourteen-year-old Syrian called Elagabalus, who had served the god Ba'al at Emesa, became Roman Emperor for fewer than four years, being lynched by his guards in AD 222. He attempted unsuccessfully to introduce his local cult of Sol Invictus, the Unconquered Sun, to Rome. About fifty years later, the Emperor Aurelian had more success when he established the Sun as the supreme deity of

ABOVE
(Naples Museum) This wall painting from Herculaneum is thought to show the morning ceremony in a sanctuary of Isis during which the high priest poured libations on all the altars in the temple precinct.

OPPOSITE
The Egyptian jackal-headed god, Anubis, is presented as a classical Greek figure in this statue from the Serapeum-Canopus at Hadrian's villa at Tivoli. It illustrates the wide-ranging cultural traditions upon which educated and fashionable Romans could draw.

Rome. He came from Illyria, where the sun was worshipped, but some of his army came from Syria, which Aurelian also knew, having visited Palmyra and Emesa. He was thus making an intelligent attempt to unite the eastern and western empire by bringing together the sun-worship of the east with the western Celtic and Germanic gods of healing and light who had become associated with Apollo. December 25, the winter solstice, was the birthday of the sun, a festival that was later appropriated by the Christians.

The Phoenicians who migrated to Carthage took their gods with them and some of these gods later became assimilated with Roman gods. Ba'al, the Lord, became assimilated with Zeus/Jupiter in Palestine and with Saturn in Africa. The latter assimilation to the early Roman fertility god seems appropriate. Tanit, the Carthaginian moon-goddess, was assimilated at first to the Great Mother, who later gave way to Juno, but Tanit also continued as Caelestis, who was herself later assimilated to Aphrodite/Venus. She was also strongly associated with Ceres.

At Corbridge, in England, an altar was dedicated to Jupiter Dolichenus, Caelestis Brigantia, and Salus. In this very interesting triad, the local goddess Brigantia is identified with Caelestis/Juno – the Syrian/Roman goddess – and is thus the wife of Jupiter in his Syrian version; Salus, the personified god of healing, completes the triad which now seems to us exotic, but was clearly quite acceptable to the Roman in Britain who could afford to have the altar made.

When Roman colonists settled abroad they often attempted to recreate the heart of Rome itself by making a citadel on which they built a temple to the triad of gods – Jupiter Optimus Maximus, Juno Regina, and Minerva – who had been the dedicatees of the first temple on the Capitoline Hill in Rome. These capitols are found in the province of Africa, mostly in modern Tunisia, which tried particularly to model itself on Rome. The Capitoline cult was often accompanied by the emperor-cult so that men could not only remind themselves of their national identity as Romans but also associate themselves with the power of Rome and the benefits it brought.

Nevertheless there is, as always, evidence to show that local deities continued to be worshipped in these places. It is interesting to speculate how far the great Greek and Roman gods penetrated through society, and to what extent they ever took the place of local deities for those people who could not afford to leave behind them the evidence of statues, funeral sarcophagi and inscriptions in stone.

Remains of a 3rd-century AD temple of Mithras at Carrowburgh, Northumbria, near Hadrian's Wall. It would have been roofed. Mithraism was popular among the officers of the Roman legions throughout the empire.

CHAPTER EIGHT
ROME AND CHRISTIANITY

One of the eastern religions that made its mark in parts of the Roman empire was, of course, Judaism, which differed from other faiths in its uncompromising and exclusive monotheism. The worship of Jehovah had already spread through the Eastern Mediterranean during the Hellenistic period and there was a Jewish colony in Rome in the last century of the Republic. The fact that Jews, together with astrologers, were expelled from Rome in AD 139 suggests that their presence was at least noticeable and possibly disturbing to the authorities.

The Jews were expecting a Messiah, through whom they would establish a kingdom of peace and their hopes were always pinned on Jerusalem as the centre of their faith. Their hopes for Jerusalem were, however, shattered in AD 70 when the Roman emperor Titus destroyed the sacred city and took the treasures of the temple back with him to Rome. Images of them can still be seen there, displayed in stone carvings on his triumphal arch. Possibly even worse was Hadrian's attempt to assimilate the Jews to Rome by founding a Roman colony called Aelia Capitolina in Jerusalem in AD 132, and erecting a shrine of Jupiter Capitolinus on the very site of the former holy place of the Jews. The consequent Jewish revolt incited the Roman army to destroy many villages, kill thousands of men and women and encourage Gentiles to settle in Judaea. An agreement with Rome eventually allowed the Jews to express their faith, but it left them without a home or a political state of their own.

Before this, in AD 30, during an earlier disturbance of the Roman peace in Judaea, Jesus of Nazareth, claimed to be the son of Jehovah, had been crucified. After his death, the ideas that might otherwise have died with him were taken up and spread by a number of his disciples. The ideas and teaching of the disciples found a reception among certain Jews, who created what must have seemed at first merely a minor sect of Judaism. The teaching then spread further afield both geographically and culturally, greatly helped by men like Paul, formerly Saul of Tarsus. He persuaded the Jewish followers of Christ that their message was universal rather than simply Jewish and that converted Gentiles should be allowed into their sect, which must become less rigid. Paul was a Jewish scholar from Syria, a Greek-speaking Roman citizen and ultimately a Christian apostle. He illustrates in himself the extraordinary range of cultural experience that was sometimes synthesized in the Roman world.

By the second century AD there were Christian communities throughout the Middle East, in Greece, Cyprus, Pompeii and Rome, and possibly in Spain and even India. By the third and fourth centuries, Christianity was the only religion making continuous progress at the expense of other religions. This progress has been explained not only by the quality of the faith itself and by the intelligence of the Greek writers who propagated it, particularly to the people of the eastern empire, but by the fact that it was well organized from the beginning. It provided an interconnecting system of clergy, formal baptism into the

faith, and help for the poor; its members formed themselves into alternative, lateral, dependable social structures that must have been particularly welcome to the poor and needy people who probably formed the majority of its adherents at first if only because they formed the majority of society.

Why then were Christians persecuted? In some cases the reason was political expediency; they were persecuted because failure to do so might have resulted in public disorder. In the early period of their existence, when there were no systematic edicts against them, they were sometimes drawn to the attention of the authorities by people who simply could not accept the fact that they behaved differently from other people, a situation not unknown today when some communities still find difficulty in accepting new cultural minorities in their midst.

It is important to remember that in earlier societies, cases to be prosecuted were not brought to trial by a police force, but by other members of society who found certain kinds of behaviour offensive. The Christians were accused of 'hatred of the human race', a vague phrase that perhaps arose from the fact that they did not participate in the ordinary religious festivals of the day. On the contrary, their own rituals must have seemed strange; at their Eucharist they symbolically consumed the body and blood of their Saviour; they called each other 'brother' and 'sister'

and kissed on meeting; early rumours of cannibalism and incest were perhaps understandable. Furthermore they treated women with honour and they worshipped a criminal whom the Romans had put to death. Some of this feeling is displayed even by a writer as intelligent as the historian Tacitus, who wrote of their 'detestable superstition', and complained of their presence in Rome 'where every horrible and shameful iniquity, from every quarter of the world, pours in and finds a welcome.'

It is only fair to note that the Christians themselves were extremely intolerant and unyielding. Unusually, they wanted their form of worship to replace other worships, rather than to accept them as equals. When they were accused of crimes, they refused to take the simple step that would have freed them – to offer a sacrifice to the gods or the Emperor. Other religions accepted a variety of gods into their pantheon; the Christians did not. They would not admit that Emperors could be divine, and would certainly not sacrifice to them or pray to them, although they might pray for them. They wanted to change the world, which was always regarded as a dangerously

revolutionary position in Rome, but they went further and talked of establishing a new kingdom on earth. By refusing to behave piously towards the Roman gods, they were abusing the very traditions that had formed the Roman character and the Roman state, as this book has tried to show.

It seems that once people knew them as neighbours, on the whole they came to trust and like them. It was, however, inevitable that the Christians should become an irritant to the authorities. They first appear as a separate group, rather than as a sect of Judaism, at the time of the emperor Nero, when Paul appealed to him on their behalf. Paul himself had provoked a riot in Ephesus, in Asia Minor, when he preached against the city's goddess, Artemis/Diana. Nero did not persecute the Christians systematically but he discovered that they provided him with a convenient scapegoat to blame when things were going wrong for him. For example, he used the opportunity offered by the great fire in Rome in AD 64 to accumulate land, consequently rumours circulated that the fire had been started deliberately. Tacitus claimed that Nero chose to divert attention from himself by blaming the Christians as arsonists and devising exotic punishments for them. This, of course, would have led to their being blamed for almost any disagreeable event in the future.

In the early second century, Pliny indicates the general attitude taken by authority to the Christians by quoting a letter written to him by the Emperor Trajan. Pliny, who was governor of Bithynia from AD 111-113, asked Trajan how to proceed when Christians were brought before him at court hearings. How should he differentiate between them? and what should he do if they had been accused anonymously? Trajan's answer was that Christians should not be sought out, but that if they were reported and the case against them were proved, they should be punished. Any person who denied he was Christian and illustrated this by praying to the Roman gods should be pardoned, however suspect his past. Anonymous written allegations should have no place in any charge.

This policy of not searching out Christians, but of trying them when they had been reported seems to have been the one adopted by most Emperors between Trajan and Decius, that is from about AD 98 until AD 249. It meant that Christians were fairly safe unless they became very unpopular for some reason with the people among whom they lived or found themselves being blamed for some specific circumstances, for which they might not have been responsible. Even then, the authorities were some-times reluctant to intervene, as they were in the case of the martyrdom of Bishop Polycarp of Smyrna in about AD 157 when a mob brought him to a stadium and insisted that, the games with the wild animals being over, he should instead be burned for refusing to curse Christ. According to the description of his death, the Jews in the crowd were particularly anxious to help with building the fire. The authorities on that occasion tried to persuade him to save himself by simply saying 'Caesar is lord' and performing the sacrifice, but his refusal to do so meant they could not have controlled the crowd without allowing the burning to take place.

Perhaps Tertullian, a Christian writer born in Carthage, was right when he said that 'the blood of Christians is seed', and that the news of such martyrdoms actually helped the spread of Christianity. In the first two centuries the numbers of the Christians who performed the required actions and escaped martyrdom were not recorded so we shall never know how many they were.

Things changed in AD 250 when the Emperor Decius, in view of many troubles in the Empire, decided to secure the *pax deorum* by proving his loyalty to the old gods of Rome. Through doing this, he hoped to restore order.

Among his measures was a determined suppression of Christianity. He commanded all Christians to give up their faith and take part in the normal worship of the Roman gods of the Empire, and he sent

BELOW LEFT
An early Christian baptismal bath, with steps down to it, typical of those found in North Africa. This one was in a Christian church that earlier had been a Roman temple. Sbeitla, Tunisia.

BELOW
The theatre at Ephesus in Asia Minor (modern Turkey) where St. Paul preached against the goddess Diana.

ABOVE
(Hermitage Museum, St. Petersburg)
One panel of an ivory diptych from
Constantinople showing members of
the court seated in an arena watch-
ing men and bears fighting at the
games. Circa AD 500.

RIGHT
Christians were among the victims
forced to fight with men or animals
at the public spectacles held in the
arena of this huge Colosseum at
El Jem in Tunisia. Early 3rd
century AD.

officials to make sure they did. He arrested the most prominent Christian clergy and executed the Pope. All Christians had to make a sacrifice or libation (a pouring out of wine) to the Roman gods, or suffer death or imprisonment. Anyone who performed the sacrifice received a releasing certificate, some of which still survive. Some people might have bought the certificates without performing the actions; others escaped, but many were killed.

Decius died in AD 251, but Valerian renewed the persecution in 257 and Aurelian in 270, so that suppression became official policy for a number of years. After that, things were relaxed and for some years authority turned a blind eye to Christians who refused to worship the emperor, which meant that

they could once more enter the civil service and, in some cases, rise to high office.

The most serious attack on them came under Diocletian and began in AD 303. It was surprising, since Diocletian had seemed tolerant, and had even married a Christian wife. It was Diocletian who instituted the tetrarchy, the system of shared imperial rule by which he hoped the empire would be more efficiently run. The tetrarchy was an agreement between four emperors: two were senior and were known as Augustus; the other two were their lieutenants, or deputies, and were known as Caesar. They co-operated closely, and sometimes linked themselves together by judicious marriages. Diocletian had a particularly anti-Christian deputy, called Galerius, who may have been the inspiration for the worst excesses.

Somewhat in the spirit of Augustus, Diocletian had decided that the time had come to bring back sound moral values to Rome; the gods would be favourable to Rome, he said, if its rulers saw to it that everyone cultivated a pious life. Members of new religions were coming between the Romans and their gods and opposing the older religious practices that had always served Rome well. Perverted and obstinate people like the Christians must be punished.

He did not demand bloodshed, but decreed that churches must be destroyed, the scriptures burnt and higher class Christians deprived of their immunities from punishment; he then went further and decreed that Christians should be captured and forced to sacrifice before being released. While Diocletian was ill, however, Galerius took advantage of his absence and demanded universal sacrifice to the gods on pain of death. This initiated the most serious period of persecution ever known, until Galerius repented on his death bed in AD 311, stopped the persecution and, in an edict, granted Christians what they had always wanted, legal recognition. This edict was also signed by Constantine.

Constantine's father, Constantius, had been Augustus, together with Galerius, when Diocletian retired, but when Constantius died at York during an expedition in AD 306, his troops proclaimed his son Constantine as their leader. Constantine was opposed by two of the other tetrarchs, but he entered Rome in 312, having successfully fought off opposition to his rule at the Battle of the Milvian Bridge outside Rome.

It was said that just before that battle, Constantine dreamed of the sign of Christ, that is of a cross set against the sun. The sun was a particularly important symbol to him because he had been brought up by his father, who came from the Balkans, to the worship of Sol Invictus, the Unconquered Sun. His father had actually been displayed on a victory medallion as *Redditor Lucis Aeternam*, 'Restorer of eternal light'. Constantine

traditional Roman desire.

After his declaration of tolerance, Constantine's greatest help to the progress of Christianity was, perhaps, his supervision of the interminable disputes about dogma and heresy that arose in the Christian Church in the fourth century. It was probably largely through his influence that the Nicene Creed emerged from the meeting at Nicaea in AD 325, for example. Constantine was less tolerant to pagan religions. He forbade any of his staff to offer sacrifice and, while he was building his new city of Constantinople at Byzantium in the eastern empire, he is thought to have despoiled existing pagan temples of precious materials to use there. His son Constantius went further, closing pagan temples in every city and forbidding sacrifice on pain of death.

BELOW
(Louvre Museum, Paris) The Roman Emperor Julian who was called the Apostate because once he had become Emperor he revealed his life-long adherence to pagan beliefs.

was therefore no stranger to monotheism. He supported Christianity from the time of his vision, but he was not actually baptized a Christian until shortly before his death in AD 337.

Constantine agreed with Licinius, the one tetrarch who had supported him in his claim to power, that the persecution of Christians should be brought to an end. Their policy towards the Christians was stated clearly in AD 313, in the 'Edict of Milan', which said that Christians, and everyone else, should be granted the freedom to follow whatever religious observance they wished, 'so that whatever divinity there is in the seat of heaven may become placated and propitious to us and to all who are under our rule,' This last clause manifestly expresses a very

The number of edicts on these lines that were pro-
nounced over the years suggests, however, that they
were not very effective.

It is not surprising that Christianity in the period
of Constantine was far more widespread in the eastern than in the western empire. Possibly up to half
the population were Christian in Alexandria and in
other cities in Syria and Asia Minor where Greek
culture and philosophy had in some sense paved the
way for new kinds of thinking. Only a minority of
people in Rome itself and in the west were Christian
by that period. It is interesting to note that the Latin
Bible probably originated from North Africa, and
that an important line of Christian converts writing
in Latin grew up there and influenced the western
empire; they included Tertullian, Cyprian and the
great Augustine.

There was one more pagan Roman Emperor,
Flavius Claudius Julianus, known as Julian the
Apostate, who ruled from AD 361-363. He was born
in Constantinople and, although brought up as
a Christian, he was actually far more attracted
by pagan literature and the philosophers of
Neoplatonism. He kept his ideas to himself during a
very successful military career, but when he became
emperor he shed his Christian upbringing and
decreed that all religions in the Empire were to be
tolerated. He gave his active support to pagan groups
and withdrew it from Christian ones. Nevertheless,
he admitted in writing that the ultimate victory of
Christianity in the Roman world was assured.

Over the centuries, Christians were to show
themselves perhaps more intolerant than the Romans
had been as they set about eliminating paganism.
Compromises had to be made. It has been suggested,
for example, that the suppression of the worship of
local deities by certain campaigning bishops may
well have led to their reincarnation as Christian

An example of pagan and Christian syncretism in a mid-4th century mosaic in the Mausoleum of Santa Constanza in Rome. The putti could have come from a pagan scene, but here they seem to be perceived as sharing in the Lord's harvest. The vine, which had been a pagan symbol of fruitfulness, could also signify the joy of a Christian paradise.

saints. The Christians also took existing festivals into their calendar, as they did with the winter solstice and birthday of Sol, 25 December.

In the light of all that has been said here about the merging of cults and images, early Christian images are interesting in the manner in which they demonstrate that their makers have assimilated them to earlier traditions. The crucifix as an image is noticeable by its absence in the early Christian period when Christians were reluctant to associate their religion with the instrument by which the most hardened criminals were put to death. They used instead the chi-ro sign, bringing together the first two Greek letters of Christ's name. This in itself forms a cross against a circle, in the manner of Constantine's vision.

Christ was also visualized as the Good Shepherd, and statues of him are reminiscent of Greek statues of Apollo carrying a calf from centuries earlier. Scholars have seen images of the goddess Isis influencing some statues of the Virgin Mary. In order to represent the delights of heaven, age-old images of the vine and the harvest were used, as they had been in the worship of Dionysus. The first youthful images of Christ gave way to the now familiar bearded figure with a halo. The halo is in itself reminiscent of the radiate crown of those gods and emperors who had been associated with the sun. Themes of the conflict of good and evil are represented by hunting scenes on Christian sarcophagi, and even Bellerophon killing the Chimaera and Perseus slaying the dragon are used to suggest the triumph of good over evil, to the extent that the latter probably produced the notion of St. George.

Discussion of the further development of Christianity lies beyond the scope of this book. It is difficult to see, however, how its propagation would have spread so rapidly without the cultural conditions brought about by the great melting pot of the Roman world. Perhaps even more important for the transmission of Christianity was Rome's administrative ability and the technical prowess that made communication possible from the Thames to the Indus and the Rhine to the Nile.

INDEX

Pages in italics refer to illustrations

A

Achilles 25, 27
Actium, battle of 15, 25, *78, 79*
Adolenda 42
Adonis
Aelia Capitolina 94
Aeneas 7, 17, 18, 19, *19*, 20, *20*, 21, *21*, 22, 23, 24, *24*, 25, *25*, 27, *27*, 28, 30, 42, 61, 79, 81
Aeneid (Virgil) *17*, 19, *21*, 27, 79
Aesculapius 61, 89
Agdistis 72
Agrippa, Marcus *83*
Ahriman 85
Ahura-Mazda 85
Alba Longa 7, 19, 22, 24, 30, 35, 36, 46
Alexander the Great 6, 16, 59, 81, 85, 88
Allecto 23
Amulius 28, 29, 30
Anchises 18, 19, 20, 21, 22, 79, 81
Ancus Marcius 36, 37, 38
Antinous 82, *86*
Antoninus Pius, Emperor *86, 106*
Anubis 83, *89*
Aphrodite (*see also* Venus) 18, 19, 20, 63, 90
Apis, bulls of 83
Apollo 19, 22, 24, 25, *51*, 61, 62, 63, 64, 67, *78*, 79, 81, *82*, 83, 88, 90, *103*, 106
Appian Way *57*, 60
Aquae Sulis 88
Arcadia 24
Ares (*see also* Mars) 62, 63
Arruns 38
Artemis (*see also* Diana) 63, 96
Ascanius 19, *20*, 22, 23, 25, 81
Asia, province of 14
Asia Minor 6, 10, 11, 15, *73*, 88, 96, *97*, 103
Asclepius (*see* Aesculapius)
Astarte 20
Atagartis 88
Athena (*see also* Minerva) 63

Athens 18, 77
Atlas 24
Attalus, king of Pergamum 14, 69
Attis 72, *73*
augury 53
Augustus, Emperor 15, *15*, 17, 18, 19, 22, 25, *25*, 28, 35, 51, *78*, 79, *80*, 81, 82, 83, *85*, 100, 103; *Ara Pacis Augustae* 25, 81, *83, 84*
Aurelian, Emperor 89, 90, 98
Aurora *78*
Aventine Hill 30

B

Ba'al 89, 90
Bacchic mysteries *77*
Bacchus 72, *75*
Bellerophon 106
Bona Dea 47
Britain 16, 90
Bronze Age 6, 18, 54, 55
Brutus, Lucius Junius 38, 39, 40
Buddha 6
Byzantium 16, 101

C

Cacus 60
Caelestis (*see* Tanit); Caelestis Brigantia 90; Caelestis Juno 90
Caere 23
Caesar, Gaius Julius 14, 15, *16*, 19, 25, 40, 79, 81, 83, 88
Caligula, Emperor 82, 83, 84
Cannae, battle of 14, 69
Capitol *7*, 12, 24, 34, 52, *62*
Capitoline Hill *4*, 34, 38, 49, *51*, 90
Cardea 42
Carthage 12, 13, 14, 19, *19*, 20, 21, *22*, 25, 69, 90, 97
Castor 60, *60*, 61
Cato 25
Ceres (*see also* Demeter) 67, *67*, 90
Cernunnos 88
Charon 22, *23*
Charybdis 20

Chimaera 106
Christ (*see* Jesus Christ)
Christianity 10, 77, 87, 90, 94, 95, 96, *96*, 97, 98, *98*, 100, 101, 103, 106, *106*
Cicero 46, 53
Circe 22, 53
Circus Maximus 37
Claudius, Emperor 16
Cleopatra 15
Cloaca Maxima 38
Clytemnestra 61
Commolenda 42
Compitalia (*see* Laralia)
Constantine, Emperor *4*, 10, 16, 100, *100*, 101, 103, 106; arch of *13, 100*
Constantinople 16, *98*, 101, 103
Constantius 100, 101
Consualia, Festival of the 32
Consus 43
Corinth 36
Crete 19, 20
Cumae 11, 20, 61
Curatii 35
Cures 34, 35
Curtius, Mettus 34
Cybele 69, 72, *73*, 77, 83, 87
Cyprian 103
Cyprus 14, 94

D

Dacia 16
Dardanus 20
Decius, Emperor 97, 98
Deferunda 42
Delos 19; oracle of Apollo 19, 61
Delphic oracle 38, 61
Demeter (*see also* Ceres) 63, 67, 84
Deverra 44
Diana 38, 46, 47, 63, *63*, 67, *71, 78*, 96, *97*
Dido 19, 20, 21, 22
Diocletian, Emperor 16, 100
Dionysus 6, *13*, 67, 69, 72, 73, 106
Dioscuri, the 60
Dis (*see* Hades)
Domitian, Emperor 82

INDEX

E

Egeria 35
Egypt 6, 10, 79, 81, 83
Elagabalus 89
Eleusinian Mysteries 67, 84
Ephesus 38, *97*
Epicurus 75, 77
Epicureans 75
Epidauros 89
Epirus 20
Epona 88
Eshmun 89
Esquiline Hill 12
Esus 88
Etruria 10, 11, *11*, 12, 13, 18, 23, 36
Etruscans 11, 12, 13, 23, 27, *30,* 35, 40,
   47, 49, 51, 52, 53, 59, 61, 67, 69
Euphrates 89
Evander, King 24, 25, 30, 32

F

Fabius Pictor 28
Fates, the 81
Faunus 22, 44
Faustina, Empress *106*
Faustulus 30
Fides 64
Flamen Dialis 51
Forculus 42
Fortuna 84
Forum Boarium 60, 69

G

Gabii 38
Galerius 100
Gaul 13, 14, 15, 18, 82, 88
Gentiles 94
George, St. 106
Geryon 60
gladiators *72*
Goths 16
Greece 6, 7, 10, 22, 38, 88, 94
Greeks 6, 7, 12, 17, 27, 51, 59, 67

H

Hades 67, 69
Hadrian, Emperor 82, 83, 84, *86, 89, 90,*
   94
Hadrian's Wall 87, *93*
Hannibal 14, 69, *69*
Harpies 20
haruspicy 53, *55*
Hector 27
Helen of Troy 61
Helenus 20, 20
Hephaestus (*see also* Vulcan) 62, 63
Hera (*see also* Juno) 63
Heracles (*see also* Hercules) 81
Herculaneum *89*
Hercules 24, 32, 34, *59,* 60, 67, 82, 89
Hermes (*see* Mercury) 63
Hesperia 20
Hestia (*see also* Vesta) 63
Homer 6, 17, 18, 19, 20, *21*
Horace 15, 77
Horatii 35, 36
Horatius 25, 35, 40
Horus 83

I

Iasdius 20
Iliad (Homer) 17, 20, 27
Ilium (see Troy)
Ilus (*see* Ascanius)
Intercidona 44
Iron Age 11, 12
Isis 83, 84, 85, *89,* 106
Ithaca 21

J

Janus 24, *34,* 41, 42, 47, 81; temple of 35
Jaturna 60, 61
Jehovah 94
Jerusalem 94, *95*
Jesus Christ 15, 94, 96, 97, *103,* 106
Jews 97
Judaea 94, *95*
Judaism 94, 96

Julian, Emperor (the Apostate) *101,* 103
Juno 12, 19, *19,* 20, 21, 22, 23, 24, 25, 27,
   46, 47, 49, 61, 62, *62,* 63, 83, 90; Juno
   Lucina 44, *45*
Jupiter 12, 19, 21, 25, 27, 35, 36, 47, 49,
   51, 55, 61, 62, *62,* 63, 77, 88; Jupiter
   Capitolinus 94; Jupiter Feretrius 49;
   Jupiter Latiaris 46; Jupiter Dolichenus
   89, 90; Jupiter Optimus Maximus 49, 90
   81; temple of 38, 49, *51,* 64

K

Kore (*see* Persephone)
Kronos (*see* Saturn)

L

Lanuvium 25
Laralia (Festival of) 43
Larentia 29, 30
Lares 42, *42,* 43, *43,* 44
Lars Porsenna 25, 40
Latin League 20
Latins 6, 12, 13, 14, 24, 34, 35, 38, 49, 60
Latinus 23
Latium 10, 11, 12, 13, 19, 22, 27, 46, 61
Latona 67
Laurentum 23
Lavinia 22, 23, 27
Lavinium 7, 46, 61
Leda 61
Lemures 46
Liber 67, 73
Libera 67
Limentinus 42
Livia, Empress *83*
Livy 15, 28, 29, 30, 32, *32,* 34, 35, 36, 37,
   49, 64, 69
Lucania 10, *23*
Lucomo (*see* Tarquin I)
Lucretia 38, 39, 40
Lucretius 77
Lug 88
Lugdunum 88

INDEX

Lupercalia, Festival of 24, 29, 30, 54
Luperci 54

M

Macedonia 14
Macedonian Wars 14
Magna Graecia 11, 18, 59
Manes 46
Maponus 88
Mark Antony 15
Mars 19, 28, 34, 35, 47, 54, 62, 63, 79;
    Mars Coccidius 88; Mars Lenus 88; Mars
    Ultor 79, *80*
Mary, the Blessed Virgin 106
Mastarna 37
Maxentius, Emperor *100*
Megalensia games 69
Melqart 60, 89
Menvra 49
Mercury (*see also* Hermes) 21, *60*, 61, 63,
    67, 88
Mezentius 23, 25
Milvian Bridge, battle of 100, *100*
Minerva (*see also* Athena) 12, 47, 49, 61,
    61, 63, 90
Mithradates 14
Mithraism 85, 87, *93*
Mithras 85, 87, *93*
Moneta 64

N

Neptune (*see also* Poseidon) 21, 32, 63,
    64, 67
Nero, Emperor 82, 83, 96
Nicaea, council of 101
Numa Pompilius, King 32, 35, 64
numina 7, 41, 49, 69
Numitor 28, 30

O

Octavian (Gaius Julius Caesar Octavianus)
(*see* Augustus, Emperor)
Odysseus 19, 20, *21*

Odyssey (Homer) 19, *21*
Ops 44
Osiris 6, 83
Osorapis 83
Ostia Antica *7*, 36, *36, 37*, 69
Ostrogoths 16
Ovid 15, 42

P

Paestum 12, *23*
Palatine Hill 12, 24, *27*, 30, 32, 34, 43, 54,
    55, 64, 69, 79
Pales 44
Pallas 24, 25, 27
Pan 30
Panaetius 77
Parilia, Festival of 44
Paris 19
Patroclus
Paul, St. 94, *95*, 96, *97*
pax deorum 7, 51, 72, 97
Pax Romana 15
Penates 42, 61
Persephone 67, 69
Perseus 106
Phoenicia 19
Phoenicians 14, 20, 21, 60, 90
Pietas 64
Pilumnus 44
Pliny 97
Po, river 10, 11
Pollux 60, *60*, 61
Polycarp, bishop 97
Polyphemus 20
Pompeii *41, 43, 69*, 75, *77, 82*, 88, 94
Pompey 14, 15
Pontifex Maximus 16, 51, *51*, 55, 79
Pontus 14
Poseidon (*see also* Neptune) 18, 63
Priam, King 20
Proserpina (*see* Persephone)
Ptolemies, the 81
Ptolemy I 83
Punic Wars 14, 19, 69, *69*, 72

Q

Quirinal Hill 12, 38
Quirinus 34, 35, 47
Quirites 34, 47

R

Remus 7, *24*, 28, 29, *29*, 30, 32, 47, 53, 54
Republic, the 12, 14, 15, 22, *34*, 35, 49, 51,
    54, 59, *62*, 64, 77, 84, 94
Rhea Silvia 28
Robigus 43
Roma 83
Roman calendar 55
Roman Forum *4*, 12, 24, *27*, *30*, 37, 51, 54,
    55, 60
Romulus 7, 19, 22, 24, *24*, 25, 28, 29, *29*,
    30, 32, *32*, 34, 35, 47, 53, 54, 79, 81
Rubicon, river 15

S

Sabines 12, 13, *30*, 32, 34, 35, 36, 37, 38,
    47; rape of the 34
Sabine Wars
Salii 35, 54
Salus 64, 90
Saturn 23, 55, 90; temple of *4*, 24
Saturnalia 55
Saul of Tarsus (*see* Paul)
Scipio 69
Scylla 20
Selinunte *12*
Senate 37, 38, 64, 67, 69, 72, 75, 84
Serapeum 84, *89, 90*
Serapis 83, 84, 85, *90*
Servian Wall 13
Servius Tullius, King 37, 38
Severus, Septimius, Emperor 83; arch of
    59
Sibyl of Cumae 20, 22, 64
Sibylline Books 67, 69
Sicily 6, 12, *12*, 14, 18, 20, 21, 59
Sileni *75, 77*
Sirens *21*
Sol *78*, 106; Sol Invictus 89, 100

INDEX

Somnus 21

Spain 14, 15, 16, 94

Spiniensis 43

Stercutius 43

Stoics 75

Stoicism 77

Styx, river *23*

Sufetula 112

Sul 88

Sulla 15

Suovetaurilia 52, *53*

Syracuse 12

T

Tacitus 96

Tanaquil 36, 37

Tanit 90

Tarchon 23, 25

Tarentum 11

Tarpeia 34

Tarpeian rock 24, 34

Tarquin I (Lucius Tarquinius Priscus) 36, 37, 38, 64

Tarquinius, Sextus 38, 39, 40

Tarquinius Superbus 38, 39, 40, *51*

Tarquinii 60

Tarvos 88

Tellus *78, 84*

Terminus 44

Tertullian 97, 103

Tiber, Father *24*

Tiber, river 6, 10, 11, 12, *20*, 22, 24, 30, 36, 38, 40, 55, 60, *100*

Tiberius, Emperor 82, *83,* 88

Tinia 49

Titus, Emperor 94; arch of *95*

Titus Tatius, King 34

Trajan, Emperor 16, 97

Trojans 18, 19, *19*, 20, 21, 24, 25, 27

Trojan War 7, 17, 18, 19

Troy 7, 19, 20, *21*, 28, 42, 61

Tullus Hostilius, King 35, 36

Turnus 23, 25, 27

Tyche (*see* Fortuna)

Tyndareus 61

U

Ulysses (*see also* Odysseus) 21

Underworld 22, *23,* 67, 60

Uni 49

V

Valerian, Emperor 98

Vandals 16

Varro 67

Veii 13, 46, 49, *51*

Venus (*see also* Aphrodite) 18, 19, 20, 21, 22, 24, 25, 46, 62, 63, *78,* 81, 83, 90; Venus of Eryx 69

Vespasian, Emperor 82

Vesta *32*, 35, 42, 47; temple of *49,* 51, 55, 63

Vestal Virgins 28, *32, 49,* 51, *53,* 55

Vestialia 55

Vetii, House of the *43*

Victory 59, *59;* temple of 69

Viminal Hill 38

Virgil (Publius Virgilius Maro) 15, 17, *17*, 18, 19, *19,* 20, 22, 23, 24, *24,* 25, 27, *27,* 28, 77, 81

Visigoths 16

Vulca 49, *51*

Vulcan 24, 40, 47, 62, 63, 88

Z

Zeno 77

Zeus (*see also* Jupiter) 47, 60, 61, 62, 63, 72, 77, 83, 84

Zoroastrianism 85

Sbeitla, Tunisia. The Capitol seen through an arch leading into the Forum of the Roman city of Sufetula.